Contents

KT-423-600

Introduction

In many countries, computerization of records has rocketed genealogy from a minority interest into an immensely popular obsession. But in Scotland, knowing your roots is nothing new. Right back in the sixteenth century, the French joked of any Scotsman they encountered 'that man is the cousin of the king of the Scots', for that was what he would surely claim. A rather more cynical view was penned in the mid-eighteenth century by Charles Churchill (1731–64), in his 'Prophecy of Famine':

> *'Two boys, whose birth beyond all question springs*
> *From great and glorious, tho' forgotten kings,*
> *Shepherds of Scottish lineage, born and bred*
> *On the same bleak and barren mountain's head ...'*

Sarcastic, yes, but accurate, for many of the widespread Lowland families and Highland clans were indeed founded by scions of Scotland's ruling dynasties, be they in origin Pict, Briton, Gael, Viking or Norman. And such knowledge was not lost, especially in the Gaelic-speaking parts, when ancestors' names were remembered through the *sloinneadh*, the patronymic or pedigree, in which two or more – often many – generations of ancestors' names were recited, and which was a natural part of everyone's sense of identity.

Such essential knowledge was threatened, diluted, and sometimes lost by migration, whether to other parts of Scotland or over the seas in the white-

Abbreviations		
	FHC	Mormon Family History Centres
	GROS	General Register Office of Scotland
	NAS	National Archives of Scotland
	NLS	National Library of Scotland
	NRAS	National Register of Archives of Scotland
	SGS	Scottish Genealogy Society
	SHS	Scottish History Society
	SoG	Society of Genealogists (London)
	SRS	Scottish Record Society
	TNA	The National Archives (Kew, London)

sailed ships. Nonetheless, it results today in many people all over the world being able to point at a particular spot on the map of Scotland and say, 'that is home'.

This book is for those who can't, but want to, or who can but want to learn more. I know that many aspects of genealogy such as DNA and nonconformity can seem terribly complicated, and that some specific aspects of Scottish genealogy (such as services of heirs, wadsets and precepts of clare constat) seem to have been designed purposely to intimidate the faint-hearted. And, given the great amount of contradictory information flying about, does your Scottish surname actually indicate that you belong to a clan, or may wear a tartan, or doesn't it?

I hope this book will help guide you through these issues, to develop a much fuller understanding of your Scottish family history. This short version of my book, produced for *The Scotsman*, includes some of the chapters from my fully-illustrated book *Tracing Your Scottish Family History* (Collins, 2008), which is intended to be a more comprehensive guide to this fascinating subject. In the full version of the book you will find additional chapters on religious denominations and the clergy; emigration; the origins of Scotland's people and the use of genetics in genealogical research, many case studies and examples and a full index, all of which will help you take your research further. I hope that by using these two guides, you will end up with an accurate and detailed knowledge of your Scottish ancestry.

PART 1

Getting started

CHAPTER 1

How to start your family tree

Ask the family

The first resource for tracing your Scottish family history is your own family. Meet, email or telephone your immediate relatives and ask for their stories and copies of old photographs and papers, especially family bibles, old birth, marriage and death certificates or memorial cards. Even old address books can lead you to relatives worldwide, who will be able to extend your family tree. Disappointingly, old photographs seldom have names written on the back: they may show your ancestors, but they are anonymous. Old ones often show the photographer's name and address, and some firms' records are in local archives. Directories can show when the photographer was trading, helping to give the photograph a rough date, and the mere location can be a clue as to which side of your family is being depicted. And, please, write names on the back of your own photos, to save future generations this frustration, or even include a family tree in your own photo albums, to show who's who.

When you interview a relative, use a big piece of paper to sketch out a rough family tree as you talk, to keep track of who is who. Structure your questions by asking the person about themselves, then:

- their siblings (brothers and sisters)
- their parents and their siblings
- their grandparents and their siblings

... and so on. Then, ask about any known descendants of the siblings in each generation. The key questions to ask about each relative are:

- full names
- date and place of birth
- date and place of marriage (if applicable)
- occupation(s)
- place(s) of residence
- religious denomination, whether Church of Scotland, Free Church, Catholic, Jewish, and so on
- any interesting stories and pictures.

Next, ask for addresses of other relatives, contact them and repeat the process. Once you know the name of a village where your ancestors lived, try tracking down branches of the family who remained there, for people who have never left may know a lot about the ancestors you have in common, and might have tales about your forbears who migrated away.

What you are told will be a mixture of truth, confused truth and the odd white lie. Write it all down and resolve discrepancies using original sources. Watch out for 'honorary' relatives. Whilst writing this, I received an email telling me,

'I recall as a boy, being introduced to people named to me as Uncle Ned, Auntie Jo, and Cousin Francis. Many years later, I found during my family history searches that none of them were in fact relatives, just very close friends at that time. Yet the oldest relative I was interviewing still described them as Uncle, Auntie, and Cousin, even under my challenge, with the result that I spent many weeks searching records for these people as relatives, and I never found any of them – but I eventually did find them as ordinary individuals shown as living in the same neighbourhood.'

The internet

Genealogy has been revolutionized by computers, bringing data and even images of records to your own home and, more significantly, making them really easy to search. Being able to look at the whole Scottish 1851 census online is useful: being able to search it in seconds for your great-granny is revolutionary. Scotland has led the way in making its national records accessible and searchable online, and the website **www.ScotlandsPeople**.gov.uk is a unique resource that has changed the face of Scottish genealogy for ever. It is your great good fortune to be tracing your Scottish family history now.

Computers are readily available in libraries or internet cafés (or friends' houses!). If you don't use the internet already, I would strongly recommend learning from a friend or joining a class, as it will make tracing your Scottish roots vastly easier. If you absolutely can't bear the idea, ask an internet-savvy friend or relative to do your look-ups for you.

There are several excellent websites that put like-minded genealogists in touch with each other, particularly the British-based **www.genesreunited.com**, though sites such as the American **www.onegreatfamily.com** will contain many families of Scottish descent too. You enter names, dates and places for your family, and the sites tell you if anyone else has entered the same details. When new people join and enter the same relatives, they'll easily find you. It's a new method, that really works.

Original records

Original records are usually held in the archives of the organization that created them, or in public repositories, local or national. As it is not always practical to visit an archive, there are other options:

1. The Church of Jesus Christ of Latter-day Saints, also called the Mormon Church, has an ever-growing archive of microfilm copies of original records from all over the world, including Scotland, many of which are indexed on the Mormon website **www.familysearch.org**. Founded in 1830, the Utah-based church has a religious mission to trace all family trees, and they hold ceremonies that allow the deceased to become Mormons, should their souls desire. They have Family History Centres (FHCs) in most major towns: find your nearest at **www.familysearch.org**. FHCs are open to all – entirely without any compunction to convert – and here you can order any microfilms to be delivered from the Mormon's Family History Library in Utah.

2. Many Scottish records have been published, as indicated where appropriate in this book, especially by the Scottish History Society (SHS) and the Scottish Record Society (SRS). Volumes can be bought, examined in genealogical libraries, or ordered through interlibrary loan.

3. You can hire a genealogist or record agent. Genealogists like myself charge higher fees and organize and implement all aspects of genealogical research. Record agents charge less and work to their clients' specific instructions, for example: 'Please list all Colquhouns in the Old Parochial Registers of Oban between 1730 and 1790'. Most archives have a search service, or a list of local researchers. Many advertise in genealogy magazines or at **www.genealogypro.com**, **www.expertgenealogy.com** and **www.cyndislist.org**, and some belong to the Association of Scottish Genealogists and Researchers in Archives, **www.asgra.co.uk**, whose members charge a minimum rate of £20 per hour, though membership does not guarantee quality. The NAS website has links to some genealogists on **www.nas.gov.uk/doingResearch/remotely.asp**.

Most professionals are trustworthy, and many offer excellent services, though ability varies enormously. Generally, the more prompt and professional the response, and neater the results, the more likely they are to be any good. Hiring help is not 'cheating': if you only want one record examined but are not sure it will contain your ancestor, it makes no sense to undertake a long journey when you can pay someone a small fee for checking for you, and a local searcher's expertise may then point you in the right direction anyway.

4. By using the ScotlandsPeople Centre in Edinburgh and its website. In the 'Old Days', the only way to trace Scottish family history was to go to New Register House, Edinburgh, and search the indexes to births, marriages and deaths (from 1855), and the censuses (currently from 1841 to 1901), and then walk round to the National Archives of Scotland to examine the Old Parochial Registers (that can go back to the 1500s) and testaments (also from the 1500s).

Since 2002, however, these records have become available on **www.ScotlandsPeople.gov.uk**. This is run by the General Register Office for Scotland (GROS), the National Archives of Scotland (NAS), the Court of the Lord Lyon and an internet company, Brightsolid. You purchase a block of credits using a credit or debit card, and spend them making searches and viewing digital images of the records themselves. Searching the index to wills and testaments is free but you pay to view an image of the document. At the time of writing, the site contains the following material:

- Statutory (General Register Office) Registers: Births 1855–2009; Marriages 1855–2009; Deaths 1855–2009.
- Old Parochial Registers: Births and Baptisms 1553–1854; Banns and Marriages 1553–1854 and Deaths and Burials 1553–1854.
- Censuses: 1841, 1851, 1861, 1871, 1881, 1891, 1901.
- Wills and testaments: 1513–1901.

  If, by the time you use the site, more material has been added, all well and good!

  Births, marriages and deaths are *indexed* up to nearly the present day, but for privacy reasons, digital images are only available up to 100 years ago for births, 75 years ago for marriages and 50 years ago for deaths, though you can order 'extracts' of these from GROS, or examine the originals at the ScotlandsPeople Centre.

  The website works out more expensive than visiting the archives in Edinburgh, but if you don't live nearby then **www.ScotlandsPeople.gov.uk** is a godsend. Besides bringing indexes to your computer, it has indexed the indexes, making the searching process vastly easier than ever before. And, because it's now possible to view images of the original documents online, people across the globe can now trace their Scottish ancestors properly. This has encouraged many new people to start exploring their Scottish roots.

  Take a few minutes to explore the site's extra features. There are fairly detailed explanations of the records, and 'Research Tools' contains many helpful features, such as tips on reading old handwriting and understanding old money.

The calendar

Up to 1582 Britain and Europe used Julius Caesar's calendar, with years starting on Lady Day, 25 March, but that year many Continental countries started using the calendar of Pope Gregory the Great, with years starting on 1 January. King James VI and I ordered the adoption of the Gregorian calendar starting on 1 January 1599/1600, and now that the year started in January, not March, New Year quickly absorbed many surviving pagan Winter Solstice traditions, creating the great Scots New Year festival of Hogmanay. Although James became king of England and Ireland in 1603, the calendar there did not change until 1752.

Dealing with written records

Reading old handwriting is called palaeography. Old ways of writing, or simply bad handwriting, present a real problem for genealogists. You can learn to read the former, but ghastly scrawls can defeat the most seasoned professional. For old hands, see G.G. Simpson's *Scottish Handwriting 1150–1650* (Tuckwell Press, 1973) and A. Rosie's *Scottish Handwriting 1500–1700: a self-help pack* (SRO and SRA, 1994).

www.scottishhandwriting.com offers online tuition on old handwriting, and there are palaeography classes available elsewhere, especially at the ScotlandsPeople Centre.

Older records in Latin can be off-putting, but you can always pay a translator or experienced genealogist. Good guides to Latin include R.A. Latham's *Revised Medieval Latin Word-list from British and Irish Sources* (OUP, 1965), and there is a useful list of Latin words used in genealogical documents at **www.genuki.org.uk**. Here are some basics that appear in legal documents:

• *Annus*	year		• *Natus*	born
• *Dies*	day		• *Nuptium*	married
• *Eod. die.*	same day		• *Obit*	died
• *Est*	is		• *Parochia*	parish
• *Filia*	daughter		• *Pater*	father
• *Filius*	son		• *Pro indiviso*	undivided
• *Inter alia*	amongst others		• *Qua*	as
• *Mater*	mother		• *Sepultat*	buried
• *Matrimonium*	married		• *Uxor*	wife
• *Mensis*	month		• *Vide*	see
• *Mortuus*	died		• *Vidua*	widow

Knowing what a document is likely to say can help enormously. Examples of old documents, highlighting where to find the genealogically relevant parts, are in P. Gouldesborough's *Formulary of Old Scots Legal Documents* (Edinburgh, 1985).

If you're stuck over a word you cannot read, look for others in the document that you can. By doing so you can work out how the writer formed each letter, and you can use this technique to decipher otherwise illegible words.

CHAPTER 2

Archives and organisations

Before you start research amongst records, it's sensible to have a good idea of where to find the records you will need, online or on the ground. Here is an overview.

Edinburgh

Many of Scotland's records are found in Edinburgh. The main port of call there is the new ScotlandsPeople Centre, opened in 2008, and housed in two adjoining, venerable institutions at the end of Princes Street, New Register House (home of the General Register Office or GROS), and General Register House. The Centre has several searchrooms, including disabled access, and offers a free two-hour 'taster session' each day for newcomers.

Visitors are allocated a computer terminal for a fixed daily fee (currently £10), or you can pay an hourly rate for expert help. Via the terminals you can search broadly the same material that is available on **www.ScotlandsPeople.gov.uk** – General Registration records, censuses, Old Parochial Registers (OPRs), testaments and wills to 1901, and the Public Register of All Arms and Bearings (not yet on the website). The terminals can save up to 200 images, that can be downloaded to a memory stick for a fee, or returned to on a later visit. Check the website for the Centre's opening times and details of how to book.

The original heraldic records are in the Court of the Lord Lyon, on the first floor of New Register House, **www.lyon-court.com**.

General Register House is one of the two buildings of the National Archives of Scotland (NAS, formerly the Scottish Record Office or SRO), containing many national and local records. Here are located the Legal Search Room and the Historical Search Room; the latter being the one most frequented by genealogists. The NAS's other (soon-to-close) building, West Register House, home to its maps and court records, is a mile (1.6 kilometres) away in Charlotte Square. The NAS's official guide is *Tracing your Scottish Ancestors* (NAS, fourth edn. 2007) which, despite its title, is mainly concerned with its own holdings. The NAS website includes its catalogue (called OPAC, the Online Public Access Catalogue) and guides to the records at **www.nas.gov.uk/guides/**. You can simply key a place name or family name into the catalogue and see what appears – usually a great deal. To hone searches, choose specific time periods or categories of record. To find the kirk session records for a specific parish, for example, you would key in the parish name followed by the reference CH2.

GROS and the ScotlandsPeople
Centre
New Register House,
3 West Register Street,
Edinburgh,
EH1 3YT
www.gro-scotland.gov.uk

The National Archives of
Scotland (NAS)
HM General Register House
2 Princes Street
Edinburgh
EH1 3YY
www.nas.gov.uk

National Library of Scotland
George IV Bridge
Edinburgh
EH1 1EW
www.nls.uk

Scottish Life Archive
National Museum of Scotland
Chambers Street
Edinburgh
EH1 1JF
www.nms.ac.uk

The National Library of Scotland (NLS, **www.nls.uk**) contains many useful journals and books, as does Edinburgh City Library, which also has a good collection of Scottish newspapers. The NLS Map Library is in Salisbury Place, and its collection is now accessible online at **www.nls.uk/maps/index.html**.

Archives across Scotland

Scotland is well supplied with local archives, business and institutional archives. There is an increasing number of small visitor centres catering to local interest in history and genealogy, and to genealogical tourists, such as the Comainn Eachdraidh or Western Isles Historical Societies. For addresses, see the slightly out-of-date *Exploring Scottish History* (M. Cox, ed, Scottish Library Association, 1999), or look at the tourist information website **www.visitscotland.com/** under 'visitor attractions'.

At present 52 archives are linked in the Scottish Archive Network (SCAN), whose catalogues can be accessed at **www.scan.org.uk**. It's worth looking at the site's 'knowledge base' that has information on all manner of things from old legal terms and old money to a gazetteer of 'problem places' (SCAN includes **www.scottishdocuments.com**, whose records, slightly confusingly, are accessible via ScotlandsPeople).

Another website useful for locating archives and records is:

- **www.archon.nationalarchives.gov.uk** – covering local archives, museums, universities and similar institutions.

Before visiting any archive, always check its website or telephone for opening times, what identification you may need, fees charged, and whether you need to book. Also, make sure that the records you are planning to search are likely to tell you what you are hoping to find out – this guide should help you do that.

The National Register of Archives of Scotland

The NRAS (**www.nas.gov.uk/nras**) catalogues privately- or publicly-held papers of many individuals, families, landed estates, clubs, societies, businesses and law firms. Its online catalogue is particularly useful for finding estate papers of families who may have been your ancestors' landlords, or archives of businesses that may have been your family's employers.

Genealogical Societies

The Scottish Genealogy Society (**www.scotsgenealogy.com**) was founded in Edinburgh in 1953 to promote research into Scottish family history and to encourage the collection, exchange and publication of material relating to Scottish genealogy and family history. It has an excellent library, keeps a register of people researching specific surnames, and publishes a quarterly magazine, *The Scottish Genealogist*.

The Society of Genealogists (SoG) in London has a vast collection of printed and manuscript sources covering all the British Isles, including a great deal for Scotland. Its largest manuscript collection is The MacLeod Collection, comprising the working papers of Revd Walter MacLeod and his son John, both professional genealogists in Edinburgh from about 1880 to 1940. Its 83 boxes are in rough surname order, though seem to contain mainly notes, not finished reports.

The GOONs or Guild of One Name Studies (Box G, 14 Charterhouse Buildings, Goswell Road, London EC1M 7BA, 0800 011 2182, **www.one-name.org**), includes many members studying Scottish surnames.

Scottish family history societies can be found via Genuki or the Scottish Association of Family History Societies on **www.safhs. org.uk**. The latter publishes much of local interest and members can be funds of local lore. Many family history societies in Australia, New Zealand and the Americas, incidentally, have Scottish-interest groups, and there are Scottish Societies, including strong genealogical elements, in many countries. The Netherlands, for example, has a flourishing Caledonian Society (**www.caledonian.nl**) whose members are mainly descendants of Scots sailors, soldiers and merchants who settled in the Dutch ports.

Most Scottish clans now function through clan societies, that are effectively family and social history societies.

Though not really a 'society', **www.rampant scotland.com** is an American website providing copious links to Scottish-interest sites, including travel, cooking, clans and history. The genealogy links page is worth exploring.

CHAPTER 3

Scotland's names & places

Genealogists rely heavily on names to identify people, and to link them together. Thanks to strong forenaming patterns and the patronymic surname system, Scots' names are far more likely to identify them in terms of place and family than the names of, say, English or French people.

Variant spellings

In Scots and Gaelic, various groups of letters are interchangeable, or pronounced in non-intuitive ways. In Scots, 'l' following 'a', 'o' or 'u' is vocalized as 'w', so Falkirk can be rendered Fawkirk and Goldie as Goudie. 'F' or 'v' at the end of a name might be dropped, so sheriff might be rendered 'shirra', whilst 'd' was often added, so Norman might become Normand. Gaelic has its own rules of pronunciation and declension. If your family is from a Gaelic-speaking area, it is worth studying the basics, using George McLennan's *Scots Gaelic: an introduction to the basics* (Argyll Publishing, 1998) – the added bonus being you will then be able to speak a few words of your own ancestral tongue.

First names

When Gaelic first names were recorded in official documents such as OPRs, attempts were often made to Anglicize them. Being familiar with Homer's *Iliad*, session clerks sometimes substituted Gaelic or Norse names with similar-sounding Homeric ones, hence many boys called Aonghas in Gaelic were recorded as Aeneas, and those with the Norse name Ivor became Evander.

Sometimes, several Gaelic names had only one English 'equivalent', such as John. Bill

Agnes = Nancy
Mary Ann = Polly
Angus = Aeneas = Aonghas
Hugh = Hew = Ewan = Aodh
John = Ian = Iain = Eun = Eoin
Christian = Christina = Cristine = Kirsty
Alexander = Alex = Sandy = Allistair = Ally
Jean = Jane = Jeanie = Jeannie = Janet = Jessie = Jenny
Elisabeth = Elizabeth = Betty = Beatrice = Beatrix = Isabella
Morah = More Moira= Morag = Sara = Sarah
Euphemia = Erica = Afica = Effie = Oighric
Isabella = Isabel = Isobella = Bella
Margaret = Maggie = Peggy
Samuel = Sorley = Somerled
Harold = Torquil = Torkeld
Helen = Ellen = Nellie
Donald = Daniel
Patrick = Peter

Lawson found a Hebridean family with sons called Iain, Shauny, Eoin and Iagan: the registrar recorded all four as John!

There were also names that were commonly substituted not because they were actually linked etymologically but simply because they were vaguely similar. This, as with the spellings, was at the whim of the recording clerk: your ancestors seldom had any say in the matter. Some common variants are as follows, but someone recorded with one variant may easily appear elsewhere under another.

These are generalizations. Local custom was often random, though more eccentric. Bill Lawson's studies of the Hebrides show that Bethag was Anglicized to Rebecca in Harris, and to Betty or Betsy in Lewis, except for the Lewis parish of Lochs, where the registrar translated Bethag as Sophie. He knows, therefore, that a migrant family from Lewis who used the name Sophie was probably from Lochs.

Girls' names were often created using their fathers'. Some names, like Nicholas and Christian, were given to girls unaltered: others had '-ina' added. William's daughter might be Wilhelmina (the GROS website noted the spelling 'William All-Mina' in Morton in 1769). Alexander's daughter became Alexandrina. A real Alexandrina I know of called herself Alice instead, whilst some girls just ended up being nicknamed 'Ina'. Pity poor Johnina Samuelina, who was named after both her grandfathers!

Middle names

Scots rarely used these before the nineteenth century. When the custom spread, Scots sometimes used the names of wealthy patrons or benefactors as middle names, but more normally used existing family forenames and surnames, thereby helping identify the wider ramifications of the family tree. Walter Hooks (1847–1915), pattern-maker of Ardrossan, Ayrshire, for example, called one daughter Mary MacClandish Hooks, the middle name being her mother's maiden name, and another Sarah Boag Hooks, Sarah Boag having been the full name of his father's third wife.

Those names were usually bestowed informally: when men appear in records such as tax lists or ships' manifests with a middle name, this will often be the father's forename, put there to tell different people apart. John Donald MacDonald and John Neil MacDonald probably weren't baptized with their middle names – they were just the sons of Donald MacDonald and Neil MacDonald respectively.

Naming patterns

Scots families often followed strict rules about naming children.

If this practice was followed strictly, and you know the names of all the children in the family, you can work out what the grandparents' names would have been. Unfortunately, you will seldom know for sure who the eldest son was, and the system was not followed perfectly: in some families, the eldest son was named after the *maternal* grandfather, and if a child with a particular family name died, a sibling born later might be given the same one.

Problems arose when two grandparents had the same name. If both grandfathers were called Roderick, did you name your second son Roderick, as well as the first? Sometimes no, sometimes yes, though in such cases the second Roderick might be given a completely different nickname.

Naming patterns mean that first names stayed in families, but could migrate down through female lines. Unusual forenames can provide clues to ancestry: the forename Sorley is very rare in Harris, and according to Bill Lawson pretty much everyone with that name is descended one way or another from Sorley MacAulay, one of two MacAulay brothers who settled at Greosabhagh in 1780.

Surnames

When you encounter an ancestral surname, look it up in a reliable surname dictionary. Though far from perfect, the best starting-point is G.F. Black's *The Surnames of Scotland, Their Origin, Meaning, and History* (New York Public Library, 1946). Some areas have specialist dictionaries, such as G. Lamb's *Orkney Surnames* (Paul Harris Publishing, 1978).

It makes no sense trying to research a family line without seeing if the surname identifies a likely place or origin. You may never be able to trace back all the generations to that place, but at least you will know where the line is *likely* to have come from. Kinloch or Kinnock, for example, comes from Co. Fife, so a family of that name living in Inverness is *likely* to have migrated from the south, and any in Glasgow are likely to have moved from the east. Black is good at identifying surnames that can have more than one origin, thus helping you not to make unfounded assumptions.

Derivations

Most Scottish surnames, like so many others in the world, are from the following sources:

- From the father (patronymics – see below).
- From the occupation (metonymics), such as Mac an t-Saoir, 'son of the carpenter', Anglicized as MacIntyre.
- From nicknames (sobriquets), such as Cameron, from *cam shron*, 'crooked nose', the nickname of a clan chief of unknown origin.
- From places. Some families named from their landholdings have earlier, known ancestry, whilst others come into our ken already identified by their place of residence, and no more, such as:

  Brodie: from Brodie (Brothac) in Moray (probably Pictish)

  Colquhoun: from the Barony of Colquhoun, Dumbartonshire, descended from Humphrey de Kilpatrick

  Erskine: from the Barony of Erskine, Renfrew

Forbes: from Forbes, Aberdeen
Innes: from Innes, Moray, descended from
one Berowald in 1160
Menzies: from 'Meyners', a Lowland
surname borne by a family thought to be of
Gaelic origin
Urquhart from Urquhart on the Cromarty Firth.

Patronymics

'Mac' followed by a personal name means 'son of x'. This patronymic is the commonest form of Scottish surname. MacLaren, for example, means 'son of Laren'. There are often traditions associated with the original namesake: Laren was an abbot of Achtow in Balquhidder, and the MacArthur's original Arthur was said to be King Arthur himself: an unlikely tale! But in many cases, the namesake belongs to one of the genuine, ancient, interconnected pedigrees of the Viking and Dalriadan kings, thus turning a mere surname into the key to a vast amount of early genealogical lore.

The Gaelic 'Mac' is one of a handful of words common to languages worldwide, that may have been part of the original tongue of our earliest human ancestors. It appears, for example, in native American tongues as *make* ('son'); in New Guinea as *mak* ('child'); and in Tamil as *maka* ('child'). When you address someone as 'Mac', you're using a word that, in all probability, your 180,000 x great-grandparents would have understood. M' and Mc are contractions of Mac, found in both Ireland and Scotland – it is a myth that Scots only used Mc and the Irish Mac: the spellings are completely interchangeable in both countries.

People might use one or more patronymic. If Angus's father Donald was the son of Ewan, then he became Angus Mac Donald Mac Ewan. In proper Gaelic, the second and subsequent 'Mac's are in the genitive case, so are spelled 'Mhic' and pronounced 'Vic', and are sometimes transliterated thus too. So, you may find Angus mac Donald mhic Ewan, or Angus mac Donald vic Ewan, all meaning 'Angus son of Donald son of Ewan'. Throw in some mishearing and Gaelic renderings of the names, and you may have to spend some time deciphering: a rental from Rodel, Harris, in 1690 names Angus Mc Coill vic Ewine, which Bill Lawson translates as 'Angus MacDhomhnaill mhic Eoghainn', i.e. Angus son of Donald the son of Ewen.

Sometimes, the system isn't quite so clear as this, and there are cases where someone's 'patronymic' will actually be the name of the person who brought him up, not his real father: all such cases where a foster-child takes its foster-father's surname are confusing to genealogists.

Women had patronymics too: the female form of 'Mac' was 'Nic' or 'Ni'n'. Angus's sister Morag may have been recorded as Morag ni'n Donald nic Ewan.

At this point you are probably thinking, 'This is confusing because MacEwan is a surname, but you are saying here that it can also be simply a description of someone's father or grandfather. So, was Donald Mac Ewan surnamed MacEwan, or simply the son of someone called Ewan?'

I'm afraid the system didn't distinguish between the two, mainly because hereditary surnames arose in an entirely informal way in the first place. The MacEwan Clan descends from Ewan of Otter, Co. Argyll, who lived in the thirteenth century. His sons used Mac Ewan as a patronymic that also became a fixed surname. The male-line descendants had their own patronymics – Ian son of Dougal, etc. – and at the end of their list of ancestors they might or might not add their surname. Ian Mac Dougal Mac Ewan might be Ian son of Dougal of Clan MacEwan clan, or simply someone who, as in our example above, was the grandson of a man called Ewan.

Worse, some patronymic surnames have come to be spelled in a certain way. The Clan MacKenzie are descended from a fourteenth-century Kenneth (Choinnich), who in turn descended from Gilleon na h-Airde, ancestor of the O'Beolan earls of Ross. Unfortunately, some registrars, knowing this and hearing someone saying that their father happened to be called Kenneth, would put them down as 'MacKenzie', when they weren't of the Clan MacKenzie at all. A man whose father was a carpenter might be recorded as the literal translation, MacIntyre, even though he was not a member of the great Clan MacIntyre.

There is no easy solution, but there are some routes through the mire. In general, it's sensible to assume that people using what appears to be a surname did so because it actually was their surname, particularly if that surname was common in the area. You just have to be prepared for the possibility that your research may reveal this not to have been the case.

Married surnames

The modern English custom of women automatically adopting their husband's name on marriage spread into Scotland by the nineteenth century, and was used (or imposed) almost universally in the census returns, but in many other records you'll find the older custom of women keeping their maiden name. Thus, Robbie Burns' wife was known as Jean Armour, not Jean Burns. Even when women adopted their husband's surname, they often reverted to their maiden names if widowed.

Anglicization

As Scots and English replaced Gaelic, Gaelic surnames were Anglicized, leading to many changes in spelling, that often disguised true meanings. 'Mac Gille', meaning 'son of the servant of ...' often became 'McIl ...' or 'Macel ...' There was also a tendency (on the part of registrars) to change difficult-to-spell Gaelic surnames into more familiar, existing surnames that sounded similar, which is how some MacEahcrans became Cochranes, and some O'Brolachans are now Brodies. Some surnames were subject to (almost) literal translations: some MacIntyres ('son of the carpenter') are now called Wright, for wrights crafted things.

Nicknames

Where a surname was very common, families might add an extra nickname or 'tee name'. In her excellent *Scottish Family Tree Detective* (Manchester University Press, 2006), Rosemary Bigwood notes some north-east coast families being known by their surname followed by the name of their fishing boat, whilst in the Hebrides Bill Lawson noted extra surnames such as Kelper (kelp harvester), Clachair (mason) and Saighdear (soldier, usually used of an

---

Gaelic place names

Some places with Gaelic names were given new names by English-speakers – Cill Rìmhinn ('church of the king's hill') is now called St Andrew's. However, whilst some names survive with their old spellings, many, as with surnames, have half-survived through Anglicization (such as Bowmore for Bogha Mòr, 'great rock submerged in the sea') or through direct translation, sometimes of only part of the name. Lochgilphead was Ceann Loch Gilb (where Ceann means 'head'), for example. Known changes of parish names up to the 1790s are detailed in volume 20 of the *First Statistical Account*.

This becomes very relevant to genealogists when an ancestor gave a place of origin in a form that is no longer used. If a Gaelic place name is given, and you cannot find it, find out what it means and see if it now exists in an English translation.

Modern Ordnance Survey maps show many places in their Gaelic form, as authentically as possible. The commonest elements of place names are:

- Achadh = field, such as Achiltibuie
- Bad = place
- Baile = township, such as Ballygrant
- Caol = strait, such as Kylesku
- Ceann – head, such as Kinloch
- Cill = church or (monastic) cell, such as Kilbride
- Creag = rock, such as Craiglarach
- Druim = ridge, such as Drumpellier
- Dùn = fort, such as Dunblane
- Inbhir = mouth of river, such as Inverary
- Na = of the
- Rubha = promontory, such as Rhu
- Srath = valley, such as Strathnaver
- Taigh = house, such as Tighnabruaich

Badnaban meant 'place of the women'; Cnocaneach 'hill of the horses' and Badnahachlais 'place of the armpit', presumably because it was in a narrow valley that does look rather like one.

army pensioner). The MacLeod descendants of John MacLeod from Muck, who settled in Harris in 1779 as a gardener, are known locally as MacLeod na Gairneileirean, or just na Gairneileirean, 'the Gardeners'.

Other nicknames were from characteristics, such as Dubh (black-haired) and Ruadh (red-haired). Red-haired Angus MacDougal might thus be known as Angus Ruadh Mac Dougal, or Angus Mac Dougal Ruadh. In the Lowlands, when the patronymic system died out nicknames could become people's *only* surnames, such as Duff (from Duhb) or Cruikshanks ('crooked legs'). Many people also became known by where they lived – Cairncross, Cairns, Cladcleuch and so on, some with interesting twists: the Caithness family aren't from Caithness, but from Kettins in the barony of Angus.

Scotland's Places

Your chances of success in tracing your Scottish family history, and of deriving enormous enjoyment from doing so, will be greatly enhanced by spending some time finding out about the places where your family lived. The new site **www.scotlandsplaces.gov.uk** brings together many of the resources mentioned in this section.

Trying to trace a family tree without studying where people lived makes no sense. Knowing whether the parish was a Highland or Lowland one makes a massive difference in understanding the sort of people who lived there. Were your people from an isolated Highland crofting district, a coastal settlement dependant on kelp and fish, a comfortable Lowland farming community or a prosperous royal burgh? You also need to know about the place to start working out what records it is likely to have generated, and where these will be found. If the area was subject to a franchise court, its records could be searched. Which commissary and sheriff's courts had jurisdiction there? The more you know, the better.

Scotland's parishes

Church reform was pioneered by St Margaret, wife of Malcolm III Canmore (d. 1093). Up to then, priests lived under the same roofs as their lords or in monastic houses, some of which dated back to the time of St Columba (521–97), the Gaelic missionary credited with introducing Christianity to the Picts. By 1200, however, 11 dioceses had been created across the southern feudalized areas, each run by a bishop and divided into parishes containing new churches. The system was eventually extended across the whole country, with parishes dividing as the population grew. The rather chaotic situation, with no less than 64 parishes straddling county boundaries, was rationalized in 1891, meaning that some ancestors who never moved house appeared in one parish record before 1891, and in another one afterwards.

When General Registration was introduced in 1855 each parish also became a Registration District, numbered from the furthest north

(no. 1, Bressay) and working down to the furthest south (no. 901, Wigtown).
Large city parishes were divided into several registration districts, and
identified by the parish number followed by 1,2,3, etc. in superscript.

Local histories

The histories of many parishes have been written up. Ask at the local
archives, look in the NLS catalogue or in *The Bibliography of Scotland*
on **www.nls.uk/catalogues/resources/sbo/bos**. Besides providing
background, histories may identify unusual local sources, or actually
name your ancestors.

Statistical Accounts

Read about your parish in the *Old* and *New Statistical Accounts*, on
www.edina.ac.uk/stat-acc-scot/.

The *Old* or *First Statistical Account* (1791–9) was the work of 'Agricultural'
Sir John Sinclair of Ulbster (1754–1835), MP for Caithness. In 1790, desiring 'to
elucidate the Natural History and Political State of Scotland', he sent a detailed
questionnaire to each parish minister, asking about geography, climate, natural
resources and social customs. He received all manner of different answers,
including a lot of idiosyncratic notes, and published the lot.

The *New* or *Second Statistical Account* was commissioned by the
General Assembly of the Church of Scotland in 1832. It included maps of
the counties and took evidence from schoolmasters and doctors as well as
ministers. It was published in volumes between 1834 and 1845. For Assynt,
Sutherland, for example, we learn *'There is no register of date previous to
1798. Since that period, births and marriages have been recorded with tolerable
regularity, but there is no register of deaths'*, and the population was 1800 in
1760, 2419 in 1801, and 3161 in 1831, divided into 375 families, and 1400 of
the population was attached to
the church and parish of
'Store' (Stoer).

A *Third Statistical Account* was
created between 1951 and 1992
and can be inspected in libraries.
A *Fourth Statistical Account of East
Lothian* is on its way.

Volume 20 of the *Old
Statistical Account* has a 'List of
Parishes suppressed, annexed to
other parishes, or which have
changed their names, with a
corresponding List of the Parishes
under which they are now
included'.

The GROS's *Civil Parish Map
Index* shows the 871 current
civil parishes (descendants of
the old ecclesiastical parishes).
An online version is at
**www.scrol.gov.uk/scrol/me
tadata/maps/Scotland%20-
%20Civil%20 Parishes.pdf**.
*The Registration districts of
Scotland from 1855*, for sale at
the ScotlandsPeople Centre,
catalogues the changes that
have been made to registration
districts since 1855.

Groome and Lewis

Francis H. Groome's *Ordnance Gazetteer of Scotland* was compiled between 1882 and 1885. It is always worth checking since it states which presbytery and synod assemblies covered each parish, and will help you sort out places with the same name. It is online at **www.visionofbritain.org** and at the *Gazetteer for Scotland*, **www.geo.ed.ac.uk/scotgaz/gaztitle.html**.

Samuel Lewis's *A Topographical Dictionary of Scotland* (1846) is online at **www.british-history.ac.uk/source.aspx?pubid=308**.

Obscure place names

These can present a problem if their location is not clear from the records. If even a 'Google' search yields nothing, try the place name indexes in the *Register of the Great Seal of Scotland* (1306–1659); the sasine abridgements, or documents of land grants, (1781–1830), or enquire at Edinburgh University's School of Scottish Studies, which has records down to the level of individual field names. The GROS *Index of Scottish Place Names* is helpful, as is L.R. Timperley's *A Directory of Landownership in Scotland* c.1770 (SRS, 1976).

Maps

These are splendid ways of looking down on your ancestors' world, to see what the terrain was like, what roads, rivers and railways there were, what other parishes were nearby – and perhaps even spot their actual houses.

All local archives and histories will help here. Reference books often say you will sometimes find detailed local maps in estate records, records of railway and canal companies, and processes of the Court of Session (as detailed in *Descriptive List of Plans in the Scottish Record Office*) – but few people have time

Useful websites

- **www.genuki.org.uk** (Genuki) is a free website for United Kingdom genealogy. Its Scottish section (**www.genuki.org.uk/big/sct/**) can be searched by topic or by county. It presents a map of the pre-1890s counties and, by clicking on the county name, you will be given a brief description, a list of parishes, links to the county's Family History Society, archives and libraries, notes on special resources, and links to relevant sections of GenWeb, a worldwide network of genealogists.
- **www.ambaile.org.uk**. The Highland Council Archive Service's resources website (for the Highlands) containing old pictures, postcards, newspaper articles, personal family photographs and items of oral history.
- **www.scotlandgenweb.org** is the homepage of the Scotland GenWeb project. This volunteer-run service provides county-by-county pages of links to sites concerning families, places and topics, and is well worth exploring.

to search these, and many already appear in local history books. But do look at
the National Library of Scotland's map collection, in Edinburgh, or at its
fabulous site, **www.nls.uk/maps/index.html**. This includes the earliest
surviving detailed maps of Scotland, by Timothy Pont, made about 1583–96,
which come with textual descriptions of places (see **www.nls.uk/pont/
generalnew.html**). Of the island of Raasay, for example, Pont wrote:
*'Raasa ane Ile neer the Skye upon 4 myle long perteyning to Mac-Gillichallum Rasa
of the hous of Lewis of old, now holds this Ile of the Earle Seafort, it hath ane paroch
kirk Kilmaluag, one castell called Breokill. hard by is Rona, a smal Ile, pertyning to
that gentleman also.'*

You can study the subject of old maps in *A Guide to the Early Maps of Scotland
to 1850* (Scottish Royal Geographical Society, 1973).

The Pont maps were saved from almost certain oblivion by Sir James Balfour
of Denmilne, Fife (c.1590s–1657), Lord Lyon King of Arms, whose third wife
Margaret Arnot of Ferny was a distant cousin of mine. He assembled an important
collection of old manuscripts on Scottish history, which is now in the NLS.

The Ordnance Survey

One of the finest graphic sources for your family history, often showing your
family's actual homes, are Ordnance Survey maps. Many, both current and
historical (dating back over the last two hundred years), are found at local
archives.

The Survey was sparked by Bonnie Prince Charlie's rebellion, known as the
'45, when King George II's generals realized they had no serviceable maps of
the realm (those that existed stopped at county boundaries, so were useless
for military purposes). Between 1747 and 1755 William Roy of the Royal
Engineers organized a survey of Scotland, and in 1791 the creation of accurate
topographical maps of all Britain began. The Trigonometrical Survey, renamed
the Ordnance Survey, created maps to different scales; the most detailed (such
as the 1:25,000 Explorer series) will show the shapes of fields and general
shape of buildings in the countryside, and the town plans go to sufficient scale
to see door steps and bay windows.

It's hard to date the maps to specific years. A map 'of 1880' may have been
surveyed a decade before. Some maps showing railways are actually much
older maps with new railway lines engraved over the top. This is not a problem
if you are aware of the issues and take time to find out the history of the
particular map you are studying. For help contact The Ordnance Survey's
Library (Room C454, Ordnance Survey, Romsey Road, Southampton, SO16
4GU, 0845 605 0505, **www.ordnancesurvey.co.uk**). See also **www.Old-
Maps.co.uk**, where you can search and zoom in on Britain's Ordnance Survey
County Series, 1:10,560 scale, First Edition maps (surveyed from 1846–99).

PART 2

The main records

Scotland is leading the way in making genealogical records available to the public online. With material from national and many local archives now accessible through the internet, and often very simply searchable as a result, it has never been easier to research Scottish family history. This section guides you through the many types of records that can be searched either online or in the archives, and that will reveal fascinating details about your ancestors' lives.

CHAPTER 4

- -

General Registration

You've quizzed your elderly relatives, perhaps found some new ones, and have learned about the places where your known family lived. The next step is to start original research.

General Registration records

Most developed countries have a system of compulsory civil registration (sometimes called General Registration) of births, marriages and deaths. Scottish General Registration started on 1 January 1855 (it began in 1837 in England and Wales, and in 1864 in Ireland, except for Protestant marriages that date from 1845).

Scotland's registration districts were based on existing parish boundaries, each with a local registrar, who was usually the local schoolmaster or doctor. All births had to be registered with him within twenty days, marriages within three days and deaths within eight days. The local registrars kept their own records, but sent copies to the GROS in Edinburgh, where full indexes were compiled from them all.

As registration districts equated to parishes, it's easy to search for events taking place where you expect them to be. What may throw you are events being registered in unexpected locations. Some couples married away from their home parishes, children could be born at their mother's mother's home, and some people died in hospital, or on holiday, far from their normal home. When searching, you can nominate the registration district you want, but if the search does not work then choose 'all districts'.

This 'solution' can create a new problem – a massive list of possibilities. If you know the area well, you'll be able to spot local parishes easily; if not, you may be faced with a list of places you've never heard of before. ScotlandsPeople helpfully includes the registration district's county, and the GROS's official list at **www.gro-scotland.gov.uk/famrec/list-of-parishes-registration-districts.html** identifies the county or burgh in which the registration district lies, and its start date. It's also easy to look them up on **www.maps.google.co.uk/**.

Access to the records
The records at the ScotlandsPeople Centre have all been digitized under the DIGROS ('Digital Imaging of the Genealogical Records of Scotland's people') project. These images can be viewed (for a fee) on the ScotlandsPeople website or at the ScotlandsPeople Centre, where you can also see images of recent records (births for the last 100 years, marriages for the last 75 and deaths for the last 50) that cannot be viewed on the website.

Alternatively you can visit or contact the local registrar who originally recorded the event – but often you won't know which to ask, hence the point of using the national indexes.

The digitized images are all you need for genealogy, but for official purposes (such as passports) you can order full certificates from **www.gro-scotland.gov.uk**.

The miraculous year of 1855
So enthusiastic were the people who introduced General Registration in 1855 that they included many details on their records that had never been recorded before. Sadly, the effort of including so much proved too complicated, so the forms were greatly simplified for 1856, though some extra information was then restored in 1861. These changes are identified below. Bear in mind that any event recorded in 1855 will be more detailed than anything before or after it. If an ancestor died or was married in 1855, you will gain useful extra information. Your ancestor may not have been born in 1855, but censuses may indicate a sibling of theirs who was: if so, it is worth getting their birth record, because it will tell you a lot about your ancestor's family.

Using the records

By quizzing your family, you will usually be able to draw a family tree starting with a name, 'Alexander or maybe Angus MacLeod', followed by their child, with a bit more information, say, 'Malcolm MacLeod, born in 1922', and then a third generation down, with much more definite information: 'Flora MacLeod, born on 22 April 1951, Gorbals, Glasgow'. You may think you'll save money and time if you start with Alexander (or Angus!), but what can you really look for? Starting with Malcolm would be better, as you can look for a birth in 1922, but as you don't know where Malcolm was born, you've no idea where to look. You're probably not 100 per cent sure that the year 1922 was correct anyway: it may have been calculated from an age at death, and these seldom take into account when in the year people's birthdays fell, so Malcolm could have been born in 1921 or 1923. Therefore, *start with what you know for sure*, and seek Flora's birth certificate. Once you have this, you've established a firm foothold, and can work back with confidence.

The birth record is a contemporary source, providing the parents' names, probably from their own mouths – not half-remembered hearsay, then, but fact. Now, turn to the marriage indexes, seeking their wedding. Marriage records usually state ages of the couple and the full names of all four parents. Thus, following our example, once you've worked back from Flora's birth to her father Malcolm's marriage, you'll have a definite age for Malcolm, and know his parents' full names, including whether the father was really called Alexander or Angus. Sometimes, admittedly, people got details wrong, or lied: if you discover discrepancies, you'll simply have to widen the period of your next search.

The next step is to seek Malcolm's birth: if his parents' names match those given on his marriage record, you'll know you have the right document.

A special feature of Scottish General Registration records, that is not found in the rest of the British Isles, is that death records state the parents' names. Admittedly, these can be inaccurate, because the informant of the death may have been born years after the deceased's parents died. But, usually, this extra feature is very helpful, and deaths should always be sought as a normal part of tracing your Scottish family history. To help you search, all birth, marriage and death records state whether the person's parents were alive or dead at the time, and in the nineteenth century you can hone the search further using census returns.

Births

Births of boys and girls were indexed separately, though this is of no consequence when searching online. The indexes show:

- child's name.
- registration district.
- reference number. Twins are not identified explicitly in the records, but can sometimes be spotted by reference numbers that indicate their appearance on the same or adjacent pages as another child in the same district with the same surname.

- from 1929 mothers' maiden names appear, making it much easier to search for all children of a particular couple, or indeed for an illegitimate child (where the child's surname and mother's maiden surname will be the same).

Birth records always show:

- child's names. If the baby's name was changed, a diamond-shaped stamp will appear on the birth entry, with a reference to the Register of Corrected Entries (at the ScotlandsPeople Centre and website). Rarely, a birth will be registered before the child's name has been chosen: these entries should be found at the end of the list of children registered under that surname.
- date and time of birth.
- address where the child was born.
- gender.
- father's name.
- father's occupation.
- mother's name and maiden name.
- date of registration. Note that children were occasionally registered twice, especially if they were born some distance from home: this was technically incorrect but can be revealing, especially if the informants were different and gave subtly different information.
- informant's name and relationship (if any) to the child. This will usually be a parent, but may be another close relation, or occasionally a non-relation, depending on circumstances. It would be unwise to draw any inference from a non-relative being the informant.
- birth records for 1855 alone show parents' ages and places of birth, the date and place of the parents' marriage, the number and gender (but not names) of any children they had already, and whether any of their children had died. This extra information does not appear between 1856 and 1860. From 1861 onwards just the date and place of the parents' marriage was restored to the records.

The importance of the additional information given in 1855 and to a lesser extent from 1861 onwards is immense. It provides valuable genealogical information on people who lived before 1855, and the marriage details can be linked to pre-1855 OPRs. In all cases where the couple came from somewhere else, the *place* of the marriage can be invaluable for working out where that was – whether in Scotland or abroad. Many Irish Famine immigrants arrived already married and had children in Scotland: a record of the latter will name the country and often the exact place of marriage back in Ireland.

Marriages

Until 1929 (when the minimum age was raised to 16), boys could marry at 14 and girls at 12 provided they had parental consent. Marriages of such young people were rare, but they really did happen. Many marriage searches fail simply because people don't search back far enough. If your female ancestor was born in 1850, then she *could* have married as early as 1862.

The old indexes showed males and females separately, though this is irrelevant when using the computerized indexes. The indexes show:

- name of person marrying.
- from 1929, the index reference to one party states the surname of the spouse too. In addition, between 1855 and 1863, brides are indexed under both their maiden name and their new married one.
- registration district and reference number, that can be used for cross-referencing pre-1929.

The marriage records always show:

- names of bride and groom.
- occupations of both parties.
- whether single, widow(er)ed or divorced.
- ages of both parties. If there was a large age gap between the two parties, it was not unknown for one or both to lessen the difference by lying.
- names and sometimes addresses of witnesses.
- names of parents of both parties, including maiden name of mothers. If a parent had died, the word 'deceased' will usually be added. Married mothers are shown with both married and maiden names ('M.S.' means 'maiden surname'). If the person marrying was illegitimate, they might just state their mother's name, but many concealed the fact by making up a father's name and claiming that their mother was married to him.
- name and denomination of the minister. If the marriage had been performed irregularly, but then registered with a sheriff, then details of the sheriff's warrant will be given here.
- in 1855 alone, the records also identified whether either party had been married before and, if so, how many children had been produced, and of these how many were still alive. Also, the date and place of birth of the bride and groom were given, and whether these births had been registered. These details were abandoned in 1856, but the birthplace of each party was restored in 1972.

Deaths

The death indexes show:

- name.
- name and number of district.
- reference number.
- ages (the 1859-60 indexes lack ages, but they have been added to the online version).
- from 1974 onwards the mother's maiden name appears.
- married women are indexed under married and maiden surname(s). Beware that if a woman was married before, her earlier married name might be given, accidentally, in lieu of her maiden name. If she had been

married more than once, one or more of her former married names might (accidentally) be left out.

The death records always show:

- name.
- date, time and place of death.
- cause of death, how long the deceased had been suffering, and the name of the doctor, if present.
- occupation.
- marital status.
- gender.
- age, replaced from 1966 by date of birth.
- place of death.
- usual residence, if not the same as the place of death.
- whether married or widow(er)ed.
- parents' names, including mother's maiden name, and whether the parents were alive or dead.
- occupation of father.
- informant's name and sometimes address.
- in 1855 and from 1861 onwards you will also find details of the spouse (or spouses if there had been more than one marriage). This is not given in the period 1856-60, though of course the spouse might be the informant.
- in 1855 you will learn where the deceased was born and how long they had lived in the place where they died.
- in 1855 you will find the names and ages of children born to the deceased, plus their age(s) at death, if applicable.
- the period 1855-60 records where the deceased was buried.

You may find a reference to the Register of Corrected Entries, that will include an entry from a sheriff court investigating any unusual or accidental deaths. These references are worth following up, as you may learn additional details about the deceased's family. Any unusual deaths may have been reported in local newspapers too.

Minor Registers

These tend to record people who were born, married or died abroad.
If you cannot find what you want in normal General Registration, look in the minor registers – you never know. On ScotlandsPeople, select 'minor records' from the drop-down county menu. If the person you expect to find does not appear, try the equivalent events-abroad records of the Registrar General in London (that effectively cover 'the British'): these are indexed at **www.findmypast.com**.

The GROS Minor Records include:

- Air Register from 1948 of births (where one parent normally lived in Scotland), and deaths (of people who normally lived in Scotland) on British aircraft anywhere in the world.

- Consular Returns of birth and death from 1914 and marriage from 1917 registered with British consuls, for people 'of Scottish descent or birth'.
- Foreign Returns (1860–1965): births of children of Scottish parentage, 'based on evidence submitted by the parents and due consideration of such evidence' and marriage and deaths of Scottish subjects.
- High Commission Returns (from 1964) of births and deaths of children 'born of Scottish descent in certain Commonwealth countries'.
- Marine Register (from 1855) of births on British merchant ships at sea, where one of the child's parents was usually resident in Scotland, and deaths of people normally resident in Scotland: and also deaths of Royal Navy and Royal Marine personnel (including Reservists) during wartime.
- Armed Services: births include Army Returns of 'births of Scottish persons at military stations abroad' 1881–1959; Service Departments Registers from 1959 for births of children of Scottish residents in the armed forces; marriages of Scots serving at military stations abroad; Service Returns of deaths of Scottish persons at military stations abroad (1881–1959); Service Departments Registers of deaths 'outside the United Kingdom of persons ordinarily resident in Scotland who are serving in or employed by HM Forces, including families of members of the Forces (from 1959)'; War Returns of deaths of Scottish soldiers in the Boer War (1899–1902); Scottish soldiers and sailors in the First World War, except for commissioned officers, who are included in the First World War deaths at TNA, Kew (and indexes at **www.findmypast.com**) and Scottish soldiers and sailors in the Second World War.

Search Tips

- Try to cross-refer between General Registration and census records. If censuses reveal an event that may have been recorded in that special year of 1855 then make it a priority to seek the 1855 record.
- Searching for the birth of someone with a common name may produce a long list of possibilities. For events from 1901 back, you can try to narrow the search by using the place of birth given in census returns.
- If an ancestor was born in the rather dry period 1856–60, see if a sibling was born in 1855 or from 1861 onwards, as then you will learn details of the parents' marriage.
- Events (especially births) taking place late in one year might be recorded at the start of the next.
- When calculating years of birth from ages stated later in life, don't forget that the year changed each January. For example, you'd think someone who died in 1950 aged 50 was born in 1900, but if they were aged 50 when they died on 7 June 1950 they could have been born any time between 7 June 1900 and 8 June 1899, so you'd need to search in both those years.
- Some ages were not given accurately, even by the people concerned. Always be prepared to widen your search by a few years either side.

- Occupations could change, but usually not by much. If the father of someone marrying in 1950 was a factory manager, and he appears on a 1922 birth certificate as a junior clerk, then you can see that the clerk could have been promoted to factory manager. If, however, you find an implausible jump from, say, road sweeper to army officer, then you may have found the wrong person.

- However, people tended to elevate their parents' status, especially after death, so a ship's mate could easily be described by their proud descendants as a ship's captain. Fortunes could go down as well as up, so an apparently implausible change from, say, gentleman farmer to road sweeper, could be explained by someone falling on hard times (or the bottle!). You need to judge each case on its own merit.

- Besides seeking Scottish death records for the useful details they provide on parents, it is good practice (and interesting) to discover your ancestors' deaths anyway. It completes their stories. Sometimes, discovering a death may alert you to a mistake you've made: if the supposed ancestor died before your genuine ancestor got married, for example, you'll know you have found the wrong person and should return to the drawing board.

- If you find several possible births for your ancestor, you can try to 'kill off' the red herrings by seeking infant deaths, for many children died in their first few years. This might just leave one possibility, hopefully the right one.

- Married women's maiden names and surnames are given in the death indexes, making their deaths easier to seek than their husbands'.

- You may find conflicting information on different documents. If so, consider which is more likely to be accurate. Say someone's marriage and death records give different details about their parents. Which is more likely to be correct? The answer is the marriage, because the person themselves will have stated who their parents were, whereas on the death certificate the details will have been given by someone less likely to know the truth.

- Parents' names given in death records could be inaccurate or wrong because the informant was a child or grandchild of the deceased and may never have met the deceased's parents. Even if they had, they may just have known them as 'granddad' and 'grandma', so the potential for getting details wrong was enormous. If the parents are given as 'unknown', this may mean that the deceased person never knew his parents, but more likely that the informant just didn't know.

- The ScotlandsPeople indexes can be slightly inaccurate and occasionally omit entries. If an entry that should definitely be there is not, it sometimes pays to search the original records at the ScotlandsPeople Centre (or try again later as the computer system is sometimes faulty).

- Not all events were recorded, but the incidence of non-recorded events in

Scotland is said to be low. If you do not find what you expect, always
think of variant spellings, or of widening the period or geographical area
you are searching.

- When you find an entry that is right, print it out or at least make full
  notes of everything on the record, down to the addresses and witnesses'
  names: you never know when something like that will appear on another
  document and prove a vital clue.

- **www.sctbdm.com**, the Scotland BDM exchange, is a lucky dip index to
  some birth, marriage and death information extracted from the original
  records. If you find an entry of interest you can email the submitter to ask
  for full details.

- For 1855–75, most Scottish births and marriages are indexed on
  www.familysearch.org, which can be a useful (and free) shortcut to the
  ScotlandsPeople indexes.

Tracing living relatives

This process involves using the records in reverse, working down from a
known ancestor rather than up from you. Start by seeking the births of other
children of the couple from whom you want to trace down.

You can then jump forward and seek their deaths, inspecting death records
of people of the right age to see which has the correct parents' names.

Once you have the right death record, you can see if they had married, and if
so seek the marriage record and then search for the births of children (a shortcut would be if the informant of the death was one of the person's children).

Up to 1901, use censuses to find out who people's children were. From
1928 onwards, mothers' maiden names are given in the birth indexes, so you
can easily spot all the offspring of a certain couple. Between 1901 and 1928 you
may have to check all possible births in the registration district.

Adoption

Many children used to be fostered or adopted unofficially, without written
records. The only clue you may have is not being able to find the child's birth
registered under the names it grew up with – but you will seldom know for sure.

Nowadays, two men who think they are related through the male line
(sharing the same father-to-father genealogical connection, often suggested
by sharing the same surname) can have a DNA test. Their Y-chromosome
signatures should be virtually identical. If they're not, this could be due to an
illegitimacy, or act of infidelity somewhere back in the family tree, or an
undisclosed adoption.

Since 1930, adoption has been organized and recorded by the state. The
child's original birth entry will be stamped to indicate that adoption had taken
place, but the child's new identity will not appear. The child's new birth
certificate, issued at the time of adoption, will be in the Adopted Children
Register, though this will not show the original identity. The GROS will only

reveal the link between new and old identities to adoptees aged 17 or over or to a local authority providing counselling. The record will also state the date of the adoption order and the sheriff's court in which the order was made. Adoptees can then apply for copies of these otherwise secret sections of the records. The amount of detail will vary considerably, but if the records reveal that an adoption agency was involved, you can contact them, as in some cases they may still know where one or both of the natural parents are now.

If the adopted person has died, their next of kin may write to any sheriff's court in Scotland and request access to the deceased person's details. The sheriff will decide the case depending on merit. Increasingly, permission is being granted for genealogical interest, although medical reasons are a surer way of securing a positive outcome.

Birthlink (21 Castle Street, Edinburgh, EH2 3DN, 0131 225 6441, **www.birthlink.org.uk**) offers counselling and help to families affected by adoption. It maintains an Adoption Contact Register, whereby adopted children, or families from whom a child was adopted, can register their whereabouts and willingness to be contacted by relatives. See *Search Guide for Adopted People in Scotland* (Family Care, 1997) and the Birthlink website for more information on this sensitive subject.

CHAPTER 5

Censuses

Hand in hand with the General Registration records march censuses. Those for 1841– 1901 have been indexed on ScotlandsPeople, making them relatively easy to search.

Scotland's censuses have been taken once every ten years since 1801 (except 1941, due to the Second World War). The most useful for genealogists are those between 1841 and 1901, which are all on www.ScotlandsPeople.gov.uk.

The earliest Scottish census of all was compiled by the ministers of each parish in 1755 at the behest of Alexander Webster, a Presbyterian minister in Edinburgh. They submitted numbers (but not names) of the Catholics and Protestants in each parish, and how many of these were fit for armed service. The results appear in J.G. Kyd's *Scottish Population Statistics Including Webster's Analysis of Population 1755* (SRS, 1955). Further statistical censuses were compiled by enumerators, usually parish schoolmasters 'or other fit persons' by order of Parliament in 1801, 1811, 1821 and 1831. Occasionally, the enumerators broke the rules and included names and other details. The best guide to these is G. Johnson's *Census Records for Scottish Families at Home and Abroad* (Aberdeen & North East Scotland Family History Society, third edn. 1997). Many have been published as part of local history books, and some appear under the parish in the NAS catalogue, while others are in local archives. Further censuses have been taken every ten years since.

The census enumerator would distribute forms to be filled in on census night, and then go from door to door collecting them. The forms (which have not been kept) were copied into the enumerator's book, and it is these for 1841 to 1901 that are available at ScotlandsPeople. Microfilm copies are also available in many local archives and Mormon FHCs worldwide.

Another source of Scottish census material is www.freecen.org.uk, containing free transcripts of parts of census returns. Its 'statistics' section will tell you how much of each census is indexed: remember, some of these transcriptions are bound to contain errors.

The 1841 census
Most survive except for Auchinleck, and for some parishes in Fife (Auchtermuchty, Balmerino, Ceres, Collessie, Creich, Cults, Cupar, Dairsie,

Dunbog, Kinghorn, Kinglassie, Kirkcaldy, and Leslie), which were lost at sea in 1910 when the records were being returned to Scotland from London.

- **address.** This may be precise, or could be a street name or just the name of the village, with each house numbered sequentially as the enumerator walked around. Double strokes indicate the break between buildings: single strokes indicate the break between different households in the same building.
- **name of each person in the household.** Middle names or initials were not supposed to be recorded.
- **age.** The ages of those under 16 were recorded precisely, but the ages of those over 16 were rounded down to the nearest round five years. Thus, people aged from 50 to 54 were all to be recorded as 50. Luckily, some enumerators failed to heed this and wrote down the exact ages. There were two columns for ages, one for males and the other for females.
- **occupation.**
- **whether the person was born in the same county.** Usually Y for yes and N for no, or NK for not known, 'I' for Ireland, 'E' for England and 'F'(foreign) for everywhere else.
- **relationships were not stated.** They can often be inferred, but should not be assumed. Two 50-year-olds of opposite sexes and a 20-year-old could be husband, wife and child, but they could also be brother, sister and a child of one of their cousins, or one of many other possible permutations.

1851–1901

The returns survive almost entirely, except for the 1881 records for Dunscore and half of Dumfries. They include people on board ships in Scottish ports from 1861, and people on Scottish ships in English waters in 1871 and 1881. They give:

- **address.** Households are divided by // and buildings by /. From 1861 onwards the existence of uninhabited houses is noted, which can be useful if you are tracing the history of a building.
- **name of each person in the household.** Initials or middle names were often recorded.
- **relationship to the head of household.** Usually wife, son or daughter, but also step-child, in-laws, servants and, if you are very lucky, parents or grandparents. Sometimes, the terms 'in-law' and 'stepson/daughter' were used interchangeably.

Crossed out?

You may see various pencil strokes made by those who compiled statistics from the returns. These strokes can make it look as if the information was being crossed out because it was wrong, but this is not so: they were just crossing off details they had counted.

- **marital condition**, whether married, single or widowed.
- **ages** were recorded precisely, as far as the person giving the information was willing or able to tell the truth.
- **occupation.** In 1891, extra columns asked whether the person was an employer or an employee, or worked alone. This is good for seeing how people's careers developed or declined, but an abrupt change in occupation may alert you to a mistake.
- **place of birth**, recorded by parish and county. If the person was born outside Scotland, then maybe only the county or country would be given. If luck does not strike with the first census return you examine, try another. In the case of immigrants it is worth looking through the pages surrounding your family to see where others came from, as people often migrated and settled in groups.
- **physical and mental condition.** In 1861 onwards blindness, deafness and dumbness was noted. From 1871 it was also noted if you were an imbecile, an idiot or a lunatic, or just 'feeble minded'.
- **language.** Ability to speak Gaelic and/or English was noted from 1891.
- **living conditions.** From 1861 the number of rooms inhabited by the family that had one or more windows was noted. I have always thought this rather misleading, as it takes no account of rooms without windows.
- **education.** In 1861 the number of children aged between five and thirteen was noted specifically, and if they were attending school they were described as 'scholars'.

1911 onwards
Due to confidentiality rules, the 1911 census is not due to be released until 2012. Later censuses will presumably be released at ten-yearly intervals.

Using censuses
Censuses have two main uses. First, they provide valuable coordinates on families, stating who was related to whom, how old people were and where they were born. They create bridges from General Registration to parochial registers and on many occasions will provide clues to finding elusive General Registration entries. They may flag-up a member of the family who was born in that magical year of 1855, enabling you to seek a detailed GROS record for them.

Secondly, they are fascinating documents of social history, showing many aspects of families at home, and how they made their livings. Scrolling through census returns, especially in small settlements, can give a great sense of the reality of extended families, and indeed of communities where most people were interrelated. The returns don't state how households were related to each other, of course, but once you know who was living in the village, you can use OPRs and General Registration to find out what the relationships were.

As with all records, censuses are subject to the foibles of their creators. The enumerators could make mistakes. Imagine the man traipsing around in the sleet and semi-darkness, venturing into the squalid tenements leading off the wynds or alleys of Glasgow or Edinburgh, trying to make any sense out of the poor families crammed into every conceivable space. Imagine the poor themselves, afraid these new-fangled records would lead to forced repatriation to their home parishes (or, in the case of the Irish, to their country of origin).

Imagine young Jamie being asked to say how old his deaf granny was, and where she was born: how should he know? Imagine Laird Robertshaw, interrupted during his venison by some impertinent clerk at his door, who had the temerity to ask how old he was. Small wonder censuses are not always razor-sharp in their accuracy, or that they contain the odd wry comment. Rosemary Bigwood noted that one household was described as 'wild couple – very' and a visitor was recorded as an 'unwelcome guest'.

Luckily, you can usually compare the answers given in several censuses to see what the 'consensus' view was. Later censuses tend to give more accurate answers, presumably since people had grown used to them.

Although you may not need to look for your family in all the censuses, it's interesting to do so – you may find extra clues, new family members, and see what they were up to. However, don't be too upset if some people just cannot be found.

CHAPTER 6

Church registers

Registers of baptisms, marriages and burials have been kept in various forms in Scotland since the 1500s. Before the mid-1800s, they are the most useful records we have for tracing back Scottish family trees.

The early General Registration records of marriages and deaths should tell you the names of your ancestors who were born just before 1855 (the death record of a 100-year-old just after 1855 would give you the names of a couple who had children in the 1750s!). The censuses will tell you where people born before 1855 originated. If you know that naming patterns were adhered to firmly, you can often speculate on the names of yet earlier generations. These several sets of coordinates together should point your research firmly towards the religious registers of a specific area.

Old Parochial Registers

Scotland's parishes have been recording the births or baptisms, marriages and sometimes deaths or burials of their inhabitants in their Old Parochial Registers (OPRs) since 1551, when James Hamilton, Archbishop of St Andrews, ordered that registers of baptisms and marriages should be kept and preserved. The registers were kept by the kirk session clerk: he was usually the school master or, sometimes, the minister himself.

All the surviving OPRs were deposited at New Register House between the 1820s and 1855 (the odd one, or section of one, turns up in other records, but the vast majority were collected in that period). These have all been indexed, and these indexes are most easily searched on the ScotlandsPeople website. Microfilm images of the original entries can also be examined at the ScotlandsPeople Centre, the Scottish Genealogy Society Library, and at Mormon FHCs worldwide.

The online OPR indexes are of course tremendously helpful. Besides looking for individuals, you can undertake searches to find all the children of one couple (though success depends on the parents being recorded consistently: children of 'Alexander and Jeanne' will not appear in an index search if the original records record 'Alex. and Jane'). It's up to you to work out variant spellings, but mercifully the spellings Mac, Mc and M' have been grouped together. Using the indexes without paying to view the images of the original register keeps the costs down, but takes away some of the flavour of the hunt, and means you will not spot interesting extra details, or indeed errors in transcription.

Defects in the OPRs

One of the reasons why General Registration was introduced into Scotland in 1855, however, was because a system that relied on people attending the Church of Scotland was doomed to failure: the *Statistical Accounts* comment repeatedly on the failure of people to have their children's births recorded in the OPRs. Indeed, by 1850, an estimated two-thirds of all Scots were *not* recorded in the OPRs at all.

Registers were not always kept perfectly: '*Any person that wants a child's name in any of the three preceding pages may scarcely expect to find it in the proper place,*' wrote James Whyte in the Dunnings register in 1794, '*they being wrote by Mr King, late schoolmaster depute here without any regularity or order.*' A singular example of irregularity comes from Ochiltree in 1704: '*Something – George Something lawful son to what-ye-call-him in Mains of Barskimming was baptized April 9th 1704.*'

Another message of mixed doom and optimism comes from the 1833 *Statistical Account*. For Selkirk, it comments,
'*Unluckily, the register of births is not as complete as could be wished, for the circumstance that people belonging to the Succession church, who are here pretty numerous, have a seeming reluctance to enter the births of their children ... there is also a register of deaths kept, not by the session-clerk, but by an individual merely for his own amusement. It commences in 1742 ...*'

Survival rate is poor: think about what an eighteenth-century kirk was like! You can imagine how much damage damp and mice could make, to say nothing of the occasional fire or theft. Also, some OPRs were sent to courts as legal evidence, and never returned.

Thus, only 21 OPRs survive before 1600, starting with Errol, Co. Perth (from 1553), then 127 more up to 1650; 266 more to 1700, and so on. Those for Skye and the Orkneys only begin in the 1830s, and in plenty of parishes you will be disappointed to find registers that only go back to the late 1700s. Sadly, in a lot of cases, the start date of the OPRs will set a cap on how far back you will be able to trace your family tree, but many of the later chapters of this book identify records that could take you further back, whilst DNA and the origins of surnames can open up some surprising extra avenues into the past: so read on!

Some OPR entries appear in kirk session records rather than in the parish registers themselves. Those identified as such by the 1970s were included in the OPR indexes: those that have come to light since are not, so might be chanced upon in the kirk session records (CH2). These will be on ScotlandsPeople by 2010 so hopefully these random entries will be much easier to find than before.

You can see what OPR material survives, and where gaps may exist in the registers, using the GROS's *List of the Old Parochial Registers of Scotland* at **www.gro-scotland.gov.uk**.

Perils to avoid

Using the OPR indexes is easy, but do bear in mind how few ancestors may actually appear in this source. Not finding ancestors in the OPRs may mean simply that the OPRs for their parish have not survived, or that there are gaps in them, or it could mean that your ancestors never attended the Established Church. Their records might appear in the registers of other denominations, which are *not* indexed on ScotlandsPeople. Also, the session clerks often charged a small fee for making entries, putting off the poor or stingy, and between 1783–92 Stamp Duty levied an even less palatable 3d (three pennies) tax on each entry.

So, if your family was from X, and does not appear in the OPR indexes under that place, but people of the right name appear in the OPRs of Y, you may have found useful evidence of their having moved from Y to X. But it is just as possible that the family living in Y is a red herring, and you may have to spend some time exploring the records of both X and Y before working out which of these possibilities is the correct one.

Searching the originals

Often it makes little sense to think of Scottish families as single strands stretching back into the past. Most people tended to live in communities of extended families, and while online indexes are a good way of establishing the bare bones of pedigree, they are a terrible way of learning about extended families, and can often cause genealogical problems by deterring you from examining the original registers themselves.

You may find the originals confusing to use, not least when the births/baptisms, marriage proclamations and even some burials are mixed up together, or when a list of marriage proclamations appears upside down at the back of a volume (and hence a long way further along the film). But using originals will alert you to some of the records' shortcomings and help you place what entries you have found in their proper context.

OPR births/baptisms

The OPR indexes give the child's name, parents' names, date, name and number of the parish, and a volume and microfilm frame reference. There were no hard-and-fast rules governing what the session clerks recorded in the OPRs themselves, so the records will include all or some of the following:

- Child's name.
- Father's names.
- Father's occupation.
- Mother's names (including maiden name).
- Residence.
- Date of baptism. Sometimes the birth date is recorded too, or just the date of birth and not of baptism. If only one date is given, assume it is baptism, not birth. The OPR indexes give B for birth and C for christening (i.e. baptism).

- Witnesses. These were usually close relatives, though there were no firm rules. Although witnesses' relationships to the child will very seldom be stated, their names provide vital clues, perhaps by linking a family in one parish to that of the same surname in another. Some of the Dundee registers state after whom the child was named. Some OPRs will state that the baptism was witnessed by a non-Presbyterian congregation (indicating that it was a nonconformist baptism).

OPR marriages

Scottish weddings could be (and sometimes remain) rowdy affairs, mixing pagan and Christian customs freely. The custom of processing sunwise (*deiseal*) round the marriage venue was a pagan one, as was the lengthy wedding feast, strung over several days, when copious quantities of cold mutton and fowl, scones, cheese and oatcakes were munched, whisky knocked back and the wedding reel danced till everyone was beyond exhaustion.

When seeking marriages, don't be too narrow-minded about when they may have taken place. Up to 1929, if they had parental consent, girls could tie the knot at the age of 12 and boys at 14. They may then have had a long string of children (not all of whom may have survived) before your ancestor was born. At the other end of the spectrum, people could be quite old when they married. Often, men whose wives had died in childbirth would marry again quickly for the very practical necessity of having someone to look after their children. Marriages in extreme old age are not unknown (for it was no fun on your own in an unheated, turf-roofed hut in winter). In the eighteenth century, Donald MacLeod (d. 1781) the 'Old Trojan' of Bernera, Lewis, married his third wife when he was 75 and had nine children by her before he died aged 90. So, if you just know someone's date of marriage, you must be flexible about when they may have been born – it could have been anything between 12 or 75(ish) years earlier!

(Ir)Regularity

Scottish marriages fall into two sorts, regular and irregular.

Regular marriages were preceded by the proclamation of banns in the parish churches of both parties, with at least two witnesses present. Proclamations were supposed to be made on three consecutive Sundays, though in the 1700s this could be reduced to three proclamations on the same Sunday. The purpose was to make public the couple's intention to marry, so that reasons why they should not could be aired. If one of them was under age and had no parental consent, or was already married, or if they were more closely related than first cousins, then someone in the congregation was likely to stand up and say so. A pand, pawn or consignment of money was sometimes handed over to the session clerk, redeemable provided no child had been born within less than nine months of the wedding!

The proclamations were entered in the OPR. Session clerks seldom bothered recording the date of the wedding itself: if only one date is given this will usually be that of the proclamation. The wedding generally took place within six weeks of the proclamation. It could be performed anywhere, in church (usually in the bride's parish) or, more normally, in the bride's family home. There had to be a priest present: from the 1712 Toleration Act, Episcopalians could use their own ministers, provided they said prayers for the Royal Family. From 1834, the *Marriage (Scotland) Act* allowed ministers of all denominations, even Catholics, to perform marriages, provided the proclamations had been read in the parish church.

The OPR will always record:

- the names of the parties.
- the date of the proclamation.

OPRs may also include:

- parish(es) of residence.
- marriage date.
- witnesses (sometimes with their places of residence and occupation, useful details not least because they were often close relatives of the happy couple).

If the parties lived in different parishes, it is worth examining both registers, as one may give more detail than the other. If the marriage did not take place, this may be noted in the register against the proclamation, and you may find subsequent wrangling in the kirk sessions or a local court. However, some records of proclamations do not note the subsequent failure of the parties to marry, so what you think is evidence of an ancestor's marriage may be nothing of the sort.

But none of the formality of proclamations and wedding ceremonies was actually necessary under Scots law.

Irregular marriages were often of the sort termed 'clandestine' or 'inorderly' marriages, performed by a non-Establishment minister before witnesses, but without a church proclamation. Even such formality was unnecessary, though, for a marriage could be created by people simply living together, often after a betrothal or 'hand-fasting'. Such unions were termed variously 'marriages by declaration' (*De Praesenti*), in which no promise had ever been witnessed; 'cohabitation with habit and repute'; 'promise with subsequent intercourse' (there would have been witnesses to the promise, though presumably not to the subsequent intercourse); and 'consent before witnesses'. These latter types of marriage are legal phrases imposed on what normal Scots people were doing – courting, rolling in the heather and setting up home together.

Needless to say, the Established Church of Scotland took a very dim view of such activities, not least because they dispensed with the church's involvement. Until 1834, despite such unions being legal, the kirk sessions often summoned wrong-doers and fined them before acknowledging the marriage: the union may then appear in the OPRs, possibly identified as 'irregular'. Some irregular marriages were investigated in the law courts, and may turn up in their records. After 1855, if a couple who had married irregularly wanted legal recognition of their union, they might approach a sheriff court and obtain a warrant for the marriage to be recorded by the local registrar, and this will be noted on the GROS record.

The number of people marrying 'irregularly' was considerable, perhaps as much as a third in the mid-1800s, falling to less than ten per cent by 1914. Besides the morally lax, irregular marriages were favoured by members of dissenting congregations, because they dispensed with church interference. Many irregular marriages did not, obviously, appear in any records.

Marriage contracts

Marriage contracts were sometimes drawn up to formalize the financial relationship of newly-weds from moneyed families. The bride's father would settle a tocher or dowry on his daughter, that would remain hers should her husband die, and the husband might settle money or land (that could in turn involve a sasine) on his wife and any subsequent children. In older contracts there might be provisions forcing the husband to return the dowry to the bride's father if the marriage did not result in a child within a year and a day. These contracts might record a marriage that does not appear in surviving OPRs. They are sometimes found in family papers, notaries' records, or deeds, or might be mentioned in testaments. NAS class RH9/7 contains 306 Marriage Contracts (1591–1846 and 1605–1811).

OPR burials

If parochial records are anything to go on, our seventeenth- and eighteenth-century Scots ancestors were remarkably long-lived, for virtually none of them seem ever to have died! This is largely the fault of old Archbishop Hamilton's 1551 orders creating OPRs, for he did not include recording of burials. Although the General Assembly issued subsequent instructions to do so in 1565 and 1616, very few session clerks took any notice and relatively few pre-1855 deaths were recorded.

Most evidence of deaths comes indirectly in the kirk session records by showing payments made for digging the grave or hiring the parish mortcloth. This was a black cloth for draping over the coffin: some parishes had several, of differing qualities and costs, and I expect it must have been quite a big deal whether you got the cheap one or the expensive one.

Some reports of deaths could offer splendid detail, such as this reference to events in Eshaness, Shetland:

'James Robertson born January 1785 died 16th June 1848 aged 63 years. He was a peaceable quiet man; and to all appearances a sincere Christian. His death was very much regretted which was caused by the stupidity of Laurence Tulloch in Clotharter who sold him nitre instead of Epsom salts by which he was killed in the space of 3 hours after a dose of it.'

Other records of the Established Church

The Church of Scotland was organized by a hierarchy of assemblies, with the parish ministers and the kirk sessions at the base of the pyramid.

Parishes were grouped together under a presbytery, an assembly of the local ministers and an elder from each parish that exercised powers similar to an Episcopalian bishop. The presbyteries oversaw church schools, the maintenance of the kirks and manses (the ministers' houses) and the appointment of ministers, and dealt with moral cases too serious for the kirk sessions, such as witchcraft and incest. Presbytery records mention all sorts of people, though in many cases you won't know if your people are mentioned unless you look. Some have been published: see D. and W. Stevenson, *Scottish Texts and Calendars* (SHS, 1987).

Above the presbyteries were the synods, all answerable to the General Assembly that met in Edinburgh. Their records are all at the NAS in class CH. You will find reports from individual parishes on all sorts of matters, making them potentially useful sources to explore.

Kirk sessions

The kirk sessions comprised the minister and the ruling elders, who were appointed either by the session itself or elected by the congregation. Though technically a mere member of the sessions, the minister (or 'teaching elder') was in practice its head, with the casting vote. The deacons, who dealt with church funds, were not necessarily members.

Presbyterianism sought to control people's morals in what would now be considered an absolutely intolerable fashion. So, following the decrees of John Knox (c.1510–72), considered to be the father of the Church of Scotland, the kirk sessions reproved and corrected faults of '*drunkenness, excess (be it in apparel or be it in eating and drinking), fornication, oppression of the poor by exactions, deceiving of them in buying and selling by wrong mete or measure, wanton words and licentious living ...*' The earliest kirk session records are for St Andrews, going back to 1559: most start much more recently. Most kirk session records are at the NAS, with microfilm copies in local archives as appropriate, although some records are still with their original churches. The NAS holdings are being digitized and should be searchable on ScotlandsPeople by 2010. In the meantime, they are listed in the NAS catalogue under CH2, searchable by the name of the parish. The records include minutes, accounts, records of the care of the poor, testimonials and communion rolls.

CHAPTER 7

Testaments, deeds and other useful records

Scotland's archives contain a wealth of other records that can be used for genealogical research. Many are couched in rather arcane and frankly frightening terminology, but the matters they deal with are simple enough – death, debt, buying, selling and so forth. And many are becoming much easier to search then ever before.

Deeds

A major source of Scottish genealogical information, albeit mainly focusing on the better-off, are deeds. Deeds are written agreements made between two or more parties, and cover a wide range of social interactions, from the purchase and sale of practically anything, disposal of property after death, marriage contracts, loans, tacks (leases of land) and a vast amount more.

In the Middle Ages deeds were drawn up by notaries, who were so notorious for forging false documents that, in the 1500s, it became common practice to register deeds in a court. By being registered, they were thus preserved for us to use now.

Searching for deeds from 1809 onwards is quite straightforward. Those concerned with heritable rights (i.e. land ownership) in royal burghs could be registered there, but all others had to be registered in the local sheriff court or the Court of Session's Register of Deeds (they are also called Books of Council and Session).

Before 1809, the situation was rather chaotic, as a deed could be registered in practically any court save those of baronies. Deciding where (and indeed whether) to look can be a matter of guesswork. The deeds registers of royal burghs are not too arduous to search. The sheriff courts had registers of deeds from the 1500s, albeit with some gaps, though these can often be filled by searching their warrants instead. Minute books can be used to make up for the lack of indexes. Commissary courts held registered deeds, except for those of Wigtown (and warrants alone survive for Aberdeen and the Isles), and franchise courts held registers of deeds up to their abolition in 1747.

Types of deed: There were many types of deed, ranging from income guarantees for widows and children to settlements of disputes.

Debt looms large, with many sorts of bonds or promises to repay borrowed money. If a debt was finally repaid, there may be a bond of discharge confirming the fact.

Probative writs were documents containing something the holder wanted to go on permanent record, such as evidence of a loan. A bill was a note written by one person promising to pay money to another. Protests (abbreviated to 'Pro') were written evidence that someone had asked for a loan to be repaid. Other forms of deed that can be more genealogically useful include factories, whereby a relation or outsider was appointed as a factor to manage an estate for an absent owner. Contracts made through deeds include apprentice indentures, business partnerships, arrangements for joint ownership of ships and cargoes, and contracts of excambion, whereby two parties swapped pieces of land.

Deeds in the Court of Session: The Court of Session, the highest civil court, has a Register of Deeds in NAS class RD. Up to 1660, some deeds are in the Acts of the Lords of Council (*Acta Dominorum Concilii*) 1501–14 (CS5), in the *Acta Dominorum Councilii et Sessionis* (CS6, 1532–59) and in the Acts and Descreets (indexed in CS7, 1542–81). Somewhat overlapping this is the Calendar of Deeds 1554–95. The period 1596–1660 is not indexed, and there are five separate clerks' offices through which deeds were registered, making searching rather hard. From 1660, the registers stop being in Latin and are in three clerks' series: Dalrymple (DAL, RD2), Durie (DUR, RD3) and Mackenzie (MACK, RD4). Annual indexes to the main parties cover these for 1661–1702, 1705–7, 1714–15 and 1750–2. From 1770–1811 there are annual indexes to grantors (but not the recipients, making them much less useful). Then, from 1812, all deeds are in RD5, indexed annually. Some archives and Mormon FHCs have some of these indexes on microfilm, and for the years lacking indexes, a manual search can be made through the minute books to the clerks' registers.

Wadsets: Any bond concerning land, perhaps offering it as security for a loan, is termed an heritable bond, of which most were wadsets or mortgages. The lender or wadsetter would acquire the land itself or just the right to collect rent from it for the duration of the loan. The borrower would receive from him letters of reversion, promising to restore the land once the loan had been repaid. The wadset and its termination would both be accompanied by a sasine, as both involved land transfer. Wadsets can create confusing situations, as both the lender and borrower might describe themselves as being 'of' the place concerned at the same time.

Directories
Directories started in England in 1677 as lists of prominent merchants. Edinburgh's first one appeared in 1773 and Glasgow's in 1783. There were some national directories, such as the *Universal British Directory 1793–98*, although its coverage of people was limited to the most important residents and businessmen. They proliferated in the nineteenth century and flourished until the spread of

telephone directories after the Second World War. They generally listed tradesmen, craftsmen, merchants, professionals, farmers, clergy, gentry and nobility but as time passed coverage grew broader.

From the mid-nineteenth century onwards directories usually comprised four sections: commercial (tradesmen and professionals listed alphabetically), trades (individual alphabetical lists for each trade or profession), streets (tradesmen and private residents listed house by house) and 'court' (originally the heads of wealthier households, but this rapidly became an alphabetical listing of the heads of all families save the poor). They provide a snap-shot of the communities in which ancestors lived, including useful historical sketches and descriptions of the places concerned. By searching a series of directories, you can work out when ancestors lived and died. Bear in mind, though, that directories were usually printed a year or so after the data had been collected, so were always slightly out of date. Directories also provide addresses for manual censuses searches. They are found in most good libraries and local archives, and some have been published on CD.

Newspapers

Newspapers started as propagandist newsbooks during the English Civil Wars (1642–9). Regular newspapers first appeared in London in the early 1700s, followed rapidly by the *Edinburgh Evening Courant*, published three times weekly from 1718, the *Glasgow Journal* in 1741 and the *Aberdeen Journal* in 1748. *The Scotsman* first appeared as a weekly in 1817 (and is searchable to 1900 at **www.archive.scotsman.com**).

Newspapers provide valuable background detail on your ancestors' individual stories – announcements of evictions, clearances, sailing of emigrant ships, the establishment or closure of factories, and so forth. Many were produced by religious denominations, and can be found in denominational archives. Some carried announcements of births, baptisms, marriages, deaths, obituaries and burials, and although they very seldom include the illiterate poor (for obvious reasons), poor people may be mentioned retrospectively, for example as parents of people who had risen in the world. This is especially true for emigrant families, when the poor Scottish grandparents of a prosperous colonial businessman or farmer might be described in some detail in his obituary in a colonial newspaper.

You will also encounter advertisements concerning bankruptcy, business partnerships being made and dissolved, and even notices placed by husbands disclaiming financial responsibility for wives who had eloped. Trials, crimes and inquests into unusual deaths were reported in the past with as much detail and relish as they are today.

Local newspapers can be found in local archives and some have been indexed by volunteers. The *Wigtown Free Press*, for example, has personal name indexes from 1843, published by the Dumfries and Galloway Regional Council Library Service, 1982. J.P.S. Ferguson's *Directory of Scottish*

Newspapers (NLS, 1984) lists all known Scottish newspapers, but more useful now are the online catalogues to the vast collections of local and national newspapers at the NAS (**www.nls.uk/collections/newspapers/indexes/index.cfm**) and the British Library in London (**www.bl.uk/catalogues/newspapers**). Use their online catalogues to identify the papers most likely to help.

For information on middle and upper class families, such as appointments of officers, officials and suchlike, you can also search the *Edinburgh Magazine*, founded in 1739 and renamed the *Scots Magazine* in 1817. There is a card index to its birth, marriage and death announcements from 1739 to 1826 at Lord Lyon's office.

Poll Books and Electoral Registers

Elections to burgh councils and parliament generated lists of electors can be useful in piecing together details of an ancestor's life: their appearance in a list of 1844 but not 1845 suggests a death in about 1843/4. Someone's new appearance may suggest the year when they reached voting age, or attained the necessary property-based qualifications. Modern electoral lists are useful tools for tracing forwards to find living relatives.

Very few men could vote before 1832, and those that could are usually better recorded elsewhere (in sasines, testaments, burgh records and so on). But the *Reform Acts*, from 1832, gradually increased the electorate on the basis of property qualifications, and these are noted in the pre-1918 records, making them interesting to study for that reason alone. Subject to strict property restrictions, women could vote from 1882. Full voting rights for people aged 21 or more came for men in 1918 and women in 1929, reduced to 18 in 1971. Surviving records are in local archives, and some are in the NAS: those for burghs are in class B and those for the shires are in the sheriff court records.

Tax lists

The Exchequer dealt with the state's finances. Its records are in NAS class E, although some early records are published by HMSO, such as *The Exchequer Rolls of Scotland 1264–1600* and *Accounts of the Lord High Treasurer of Scotland 1473–1566*.

The records include various tax lists. These will not state relationships, but they can be useful for picking up traces of your family and surname, and a succession of tax lists may show a change in forename that may suggest, say, the death of a father and the advancement to taxable status of his son.

Hearth tax: Also called Hearth Money, this was raised between 1691 and 1695. Collected by heritors, it was payable by all householders with hearths save the poor, or people such as blacksmiths and bakers who used hearths for their work. Useful for tracing the histories of buildings, the records (not all of which, frustratingly, include names) are in NAS E69 and local archives, and some are published, such as those in D. Adamson's *West Lothian Hearth Tax, 1691* (SRS).

His pages for 'the Toune of Borroustouness' start with a contemporary preamble stating that 241 hearths of the poor people had been exempted, so were not listed. The list of taxable hearths includes such details as:

Keingloss house	10
James Hunter in the Parke	1
William Hay, a smidie	1
Alexander Cornwels airs [heirs]	3d

Poll tax: This 'head tax' was raised annually between 1694 and 1699, excepting the poor and children under 16 if their household's tax bill was under 30 shillings. Records are divided between NAS E70 (under 'pollable persons') and local archives. Where records survive they are useful in identifying all taxable people in the family.

Eighteenth-century assessed taxes: Various odd taxes were raised from 1747 onwards, including Carriage Tax, Servants Tax, Window Tax (1748-98) and Dog Tax (1797-98), and are in NAS E326. They all sound quite exciting, but the records are sparse and few include many names. They inspired Robbie Burns' poem 'The Inventory', listing all such taxable items, such as

'... *Wheel carriages I ha'e but few,*
Three carts, an' twa are feckly new;
An auld wheel barrow, mair for token,
Ae leg, an'baith the trams, are broken ...
... I've nane in female servan' station,
(Lord, keep me aye frae a' temptation!) ...'

Worth a search, however, because they include many names of small farmers, are Farm Horse Taxes (1797-8, E326/10), continued in the Consolidated Assessed Taxed records (1798-9, E326/15) that survive for various counties.

Income tax: Records from 1799 list those earning £60 a year or more, but survival is very poor (mainly Midlothian and some burghs). See the NAS Catalogue under E327/78-121.

Testaments, inventories and latterwills

Wills and testaments are documents marking the end of people's lives. They provide useful details of what people owned, and to whom they were related. The people generally identified in these records were spouses and children, but you may also find parents, brothers and sisters, nieces and nephews, grandchildren and so on.

These documents were generally made for people with something worth leaving (and hence inheriting), or people in debt. The poor tended not to bother, but this is not always so: if your family were illiterate labourers, they probably won't appear here, but once in a while they might. As wills and testaments are so easy to search now, it is always worth a look. Even if you don't find your ancestors, you may find people of the right surname, who may turn out to be relatives, and indeed who may even have left legacies to your direct forebears.

Testaments were created in court after someone's death, appointing executors and cautioners, recording an inventory of the movable estate (anything from clothes and money to animals and vehicles) of the deceased (who was called, in Scots, the *umquhile*). This will tell you much about the deceased's life, the tools of their trade and the fruits of the labour, and what they were worth (though there was an understandable tendency to undervalue things, to keep the taxable value down). The inventory also included debts owed to and by the deceased, sometimes including (and thus identifying) relatives, clients or the deceased's landlord. You may find an eik, a codicil or supplement, usually an extra inventory added to the original when further goods or money (or debts) had been discovered.

The executors, appointed by the testament, were the people chosen to distribute the *umquhile*'s estate as instructed. Although it will seldom be stated, executors were usually close relatives, though an executor *qua creditor* was simply someone to whom the deceased owed enough money. Cautioners (also, usually, relatives) were also appointed, to make sure the executors did their jobs properly Sometimes, the deceased had written a 'latterwill' (also called will or 'legacie'), stating how their estate was to be distributed and appointing executors. If so, the court would produce a 'testament testamentar'. If the deceased had not left written instructions, then the court would produce a simple testament dative, appointing executors.

Latterwills could include instructions regarding burial, but their main purpose was the disposal of the estate. Since 1868, Scots have been able to bequeath both their moveable possessions and heritable possessions (land, buildings and minerals in the ground). Before 1868, and unlike the rest of the British Isles, heritable possessions passed down through the family according to strict and generally unalterable rules: where there was one, the eldest son succeeded to the land, regardless of the father's wishes. The latterwill, therefore, could only be used to bequeath moveable possessions, and even this power of disposal was limited.

Movable possessions left over after tax (cases where tax exceeded value are described *debita bona excedunt*) were called free gear. This was divided, a third to the spouse (*jus relictae*), a third to the children (*legitum*) and a third to the *deid's part*. If, on the other hand, the spouse had died, or there was a spouse but no children, then half the estate became the *deid's part*, and if there were no spouse or children, then there was *na division* and everything was the *deid's part*. It was the *deid's part* alone that could be bequeathed by a latterwill.

If there was no will, the *deid's part* was shared between the spouse and children: in the cases of *na division*, the siblings or other relatives could claim shares from the executors.

Searching the records: All testaments are indexed up to 1901 on ScotlandsPeople, which almost entirely supersedes the old published indexes and greatly simplifies the work of searching. The site's only drawback is with married women: when a woman is recorded 'Jean Hamilton wife of Robert McKenzie', the old printed indexes would index her under Hamilton and

McKenzie, but ScotlandsPeople will have her as Hamilton alone. In its favour, the site allows you to see all results for a surname for free, making it easy to find ancestors, and to spot collaterals anywhere in Scotland. When researching the unusual surname Hooks, for example, the site revealed a branch of the family I had never encountered before.

You can search by surname, title, place and occupation (there are no testaments of genealogists, I see, but several of heralds). You can limit results for common surnames by adding a forename or time-span, but don't forget that, whilst most testaments were made within a year of death, some could take years to be started or completed. You pay to view digitized images of specific documents.

The records, which start in 1513, come from Scotland's 22 commissary courts, of which the main one was that of Edinburgh (with records dating from 1514). The Edinburgh Commissary Court heard local cases, and also appeals from the others and cases for people who had died outside Scotland, or whose families came from all over the realm, who simply liked the social caché or convenience of having the business transacted in Edinburgh.

The *Commissary Courts (Scotland) Act* of 1823 abolished these courts and transferred their work to the sheriff courts. The period 1823–30 was one of somewhat confused transition, Edinburgh not ceasing to function until 1830: some testaments in this period may appear in both a commissary and a sheriff court (and will thus appear twice on ScotlandsPeople). The Edinburgh Sheriff's Court also registered testaments for some Scots who died elsewhere.

Note that inventories for people dying outside Scotland are not online, but are in the Edinburgh Register of Inventories, SC70/10.

Other commissary court records: Sometimes, although a testament was never registered, you may find that the process of obtaining one had been started. The old commissary court records include edicts. These were published in the deceased's parish, announcing someone's death and the intention of the relatives or creditors to register a testament, asking anyone with claims on the estate to come forward.

Edicts curatory and edicts tutory concerned the appointment of guardians for children whose fathers had died: tutors looked after pupils (boys under 14 and girls under 12) and curators looked after minors (from those ages up to 21). Commissary court records can also include 'processes' or records of testamentary cases, some of which, again, were never completed, and petitions made by heirs needing to auction (or *roup*) of goods immediately, in order to pay for the funeral or other pressing expenses, before the testamentary process was completed. When such records are found, they can be rich extra information for the family tree. Some are easy to look for, especially those in Argyll, for which see F. Bigwood's *Argyll Commissary Court: A Calendar of Testaments, Inventories, Commissary Processes and Other Records, 1700-1825* (F. Bigwood, 2001: Flat B, The Lodge, 2 East Road, North Berwick, EH39 4HN).

Testaments after 1901: ScotlandsPeople does not currently include testaments after 1901. For 1902–59, search in the printed annual calendars of confirmations and inventories, copies of which are in the NAS's Historical Search Room and in larger Scottish libraries. After 1959, the series continues on microfiche in the Legal Search Room. These include Scots living outside Scotland. After 1985, and up to 10 years ago, all testaments, inventories and confirmations from sheriff courts can be viewed on microfilm (SC70/17). For testaments within the last 10 years, contact the Sheriff Clerk's Office, Commissary Section, Sheriff Court House, 27 Chambers Street, Edinburgh, EH1 1LB, 0131 225 2525, **cru@scotcourts.gov.uk**. Testaments for First and Second World War servicemen, plus a few pre-1914 and some for the period 1919–38 too, are in NAS SC70/8-10.

Interpreting testaments: Not all the immediate family might be mentioned in a testament. If, for example, goods or even property had already been settled on daughters when they married, they might not be mentioned in their father's testament. Eldest sons might not be left any movable goods because they were set to inherit the land. Also, be careful how you interpret not finding an ancestor's testament. You may simply not have looked under the right spelling. Surname spellings were standardized in the old printed indexes up to 1800, but not the online version. Also, many Scots who died outside Scotland had wills proved in their country of settlement and left no trace of testamentary process in Scotland.

Most Scots' houses were so small that they never owned enough movable goods to warrant making a testament. Not even everyone of means had one, and some records do not survive: a fire at the Aberdeen Commissary Court means that its testaments go back no further than 1722. The digitized records include some warrants of testament, which were created prior to the testament itself. Normally of no use, some have been digitized where groups of testaments have not survived – but not all. If your missing testament was likely to have been at Aberdeen, Brechin, Kirkcudbright, St Andrews, Stirling or Wigtown, and you are fairly sure there would have been one, it may be worth seeing what warrants are catalogued for that court under class CC in the NAS catalogue and searching them.

Inland Revenue records: From 1796 you can also search Inland Revenue records in NAS class IR. These records were created for tax purposes and record how estates were actually distributed, and thus who was liable to pay tax on them. Whilst not desperately easy to search, they can provide useful extra information: more details are given in the NAS guide.

Scotland's Courts

The new cataloguing and indexing of Scotland's court cases means that a random search may reveal ancestors involved in all sorts of hitherto unsuspected shenanigans.

To learn more about Scotland's legal system, see G. Watson's *Bell's Dictionary and Digest of the Law of Scotland* (Edinburgh, 1882), D.M. Walker's *Legal History of Scotland* (Edinburgh, 1988–2001) and A.D. Gibb's *A Student's Glossary of Scottish Legal Terms* (Green, 1971).

High Court of Justiciary: This was the highest criminal court in Scotland, presided over by the Lord Justice General. Its cases often concerned crimes punishable by death or transportation, that were too serious to be heard in the smaller 'inferior courts', such as sheriff courts. It also heard appeals from these inferior courts.

Originally, the court just sat in Edinburgh, but from 1672 it also made two-yearly journeys, called justice ayres, to sit and administer justice around the country.

The paper trail may start in the kirk sessions, with 'rogue money' raised from the parishioners for the expense of apprehending a villain. The Lord Advocate then decided whether to bring cases to trial (it was his junior, the Procurator Fiscal, who brought prosecutions to the sheriff courts). The Lord Advocate's records are well catalogued in the NAS website under NAS class AD.

The records are incredibly easy to search, and you never know what will turn up.

Incidentally, those awaiting trial, transportation or death might also be found in prison records, in NAS class HH (Home and Health Department records). Class HH11 covers the Edinburgh Tolbooth Warding and Liberation Books (1657–1816), some of which have been published in *Book of the Old Edinburgh Club* (vols 4–6, 8–9, 11–12 for 1657–86). HH12's Miscellaneous Prison Records include details and even photographs of the unfortunate inmates at Greenock Prison (HH12/56/7; 1872–88), as you can see below.

Court of Session: This was Scotland's principal civil court, that grew originally out of the King's Privy Council. The Court of Session (CS) heard its own cases, and also appeals from inferior courts, such as the sheriff courts. The records are in NAS class CS, amply catalogued online. Cases contain much genealogical information. In 1770, a boundary dispute between Harris and North Uist reached the Court of Session, where evidence was heard that:

How to search

Under 'wills and testaments' on the ScotlandsPeople site, you can select name, dates and court. To find out which court you need, choose 'click here for more information' and then scroll down to the link to the courts map. This is actually a map of Scottish counties, but by clicking on it you are told which commissary and sheriff courts covered the county. You can then select the one that you want.

The system has its faults: according to the site, Dornoch sheriff court, covering Sutherland, only runs from 1799 up to 1824, yet in fact the testamentary documents revealed by specific searches run (as you would expect) up to 1901.

'Rory MacLeod, grieve in Bernera, aged 54 years, depones that his grandmother by his mother's side was Mary MacLeod, alias Ninhormoid vic Ean vi Gillichalum [ie, daughter of Norman, son of John son of Malcolm], who died fifteen or sixteen years ago, above 100 years old; that upwards of thirty years ago she told the deponent that she could herd cattle when Sir Norman Macleod went to the battle of Worcester [1651]'.

You will find processes, which are the writs and pleadings in the case, and productions, the evidence presented (catalogued separately under CS96). I have referred to CS cases elsewhere where they may prove useful to your research.

Franchise courts: These courts resulted from landowners or officials being granted special jurisdiction over certain lands, often in the wilder areas where nobody else was available to maintain law and order. They included regalities, having pretty much all the Crown's powers, except trying treason; stewartries and bailiaries, which were royal lands in which the (usually hereditary) steward or bailie wielded the exclusive power normally held by a sheriff; baronies, presided over by the local laird, and birlaw courts, comprising an estate's tenants, with rather limited powers.

The franchise courts were abolished in 1747, save for the baronies, some of which continued on a reduced scale. Background research into your ancestral parishes will tell you if your ancestors may have been subject to a franchise court. If so, you can see if any relevant court records survive (including registers of deeds for all except the baronies): some are at NAS (RH11), others are in sheriff courts or landowners' family papers (some of which are in GD), and a few are published (especially by SHS).

Admiralty courts: Admiralty courts dealt with civil and criminal law on the seas, from wrecks to mutinies and piracy to prizes. Scotland had a Lord High Admiral until the 1707 Act of Union, after which there was a Lord High Admiral of Great Britain.

The main Admiralty court sat in Edinburgh: for this see S. Mowat and E. Graham's *The High Court of Admiralty of Scotland, 1627–1750* (2005) on CD from Early Scottish Maritime Exchange ESME **www.maritime-scotland.org.uk**. Under this sat several smaller Vice Admiralty courts, scattered around the coast, at Caithness; East Fife; Kirkcudbright; St Andrews; Logan and Clanyard (Wigtownshire); and Inverary. The latter was the Court of Argyll and the Isles, with jurisdiction from Dumbarton Castle right up to Cape Wrath, whose deeds, processes and bonds of caution 1685–1825 have been so admirably covered by Frank Bigwood's *The Vice-Admiral Court of Argyll* (Frank Bigwood, 2001), now available on CD (along with many of Argyll's other court records). The processes, for example, contain a case from 1752 when the sailors of the *Betty* of Airth, carrying wood from Norway to Glasgow, mutinied at Inverary and refused to sail further. The master, John McConochy, had them summoned before the Vice-Admiral court, where they were ordered to complete the voyage to Glasgow, the court also helping master and crew agree in advance a fair wage for them.

The records are in NAS class AC. From 1830, these courts' civil powers were removed, taking away some of their general appeal for researchers whose ancestors made their living on the waves.

Commissary courts: In the Middle Ages, the commissary courts of Scotland's Catholic bishops had the authority to register testaments, grant probate and try cases of irregular marriage, legitimacy, annulment, slander and any contract made under oath. Three years after episcopacy was scrapped in 1560, the commissary courts were revived to act as civil courts responsible for the same matters. They continued thus until their work was taken over by sheriff courts in 1823. The main commissary court was in Edinburgh with subsidiary courts, one for each medieval diocese, and thus with some rather quirky boundaries and detached parts.

Sheriff courts and other courts of other local officials: In the early days, sheriffdoms were hereditary, but after 1747 most officeholders were trained lawyers, termed sheriff deputes.

Through sheriff courts, sheriffs exercised considerable power in running the county. This was increased in 1823, when they were given control of the local commissary court business, and in 1830 when they took over the Admiralty courts. They continue to this day.

Sheriff court records are all at NAS in class SC, except those for Orkney and Shetland, which are still in those islands. Each sheriff court had a repertory of different records, of which the most useful for us are registers of deeds, protests, services of heirs and commissary records. These divisions are indicated in the NAS catalogue.

Besides the sheriffs, there were several other wielders of local power. Commissioners of supply were appointed from amongst local landowners between 1667 and 1889, to collect cess (land tax). You may encounter their records at the NAS and in local council records. From the eighteenth century each county had a lord lieutenant who oversaw the raising of militias, and whose records sometimes turn up in sheriff court or burgh records. Justices of the peace were instituted by James VI in 1587, and abolished in 1975. They exercised criminal and civil authority in the shires, with a brief covering poaching, local crime, vagrancy, debt, raising local militias, recruiting for the army, looking after roads and bridges, debt, licensing those making spirits and tracking down those without licences. Their records are divided between the NAS (class JP) and local archives. Searching the records is usually a 'lucky dip', but elsewhere in this book I have identified circumstances in which their records may come in useful.

PART 3

How they lived

Scotland in the past was predominantly a rural country, and most of our Scottish ancestors earned their living off the land. Others, however, were prosperous merchants or craftsmen living in the towns or burghs. This section will give you an understanding of the ways your ancestors lived, and will also point you in the direction of the many records that were created by what people did.

CHAPTER 8

What people did

Knowing what ancestors did for a living makes them easier to envisage as real people, rather than just names. In many cases their work, whether in a high-flying profession or in subsistence farming, generated records that you can use to find out more about them and who their ancestors were.

There are several published biographical dictionaries for many of the highest skilled trades (such as clockmakers) and the professions. For architects, for example, there is H.A. Colvin's *A biographical dictionary of British architects 1600–1840* (Yale University Press, third edn, 1995), A. Felstead, J. Franklin and L. Pinfield's *Dictionary of British Architects 1834–1900* (Mansel Publishing, 1993) and the *Dictionary of Scottish Architects* at **www.codexgeo.co.uk/dsa/index.php**.

If your ancestor had a distinctive job, it is worth exploring the catalogue of the NLS to see what may be available. In many cases D.R. Torrance's *Scottish*

Trades, Professions, Vital Records and Directories (Scottish Association of Family History Societies, 1998) is helpful for finding records here and elsewhere.

Old occupational terms can be confusing to modern ears. A shoemaker is obvious, but cordiners (the Scots form of cordwainer) were so-called because they made boots and shoes from superior leather, originally leather from Cordoba, Spain. Another uncommon term is hecklemakers, who made heckles, which were toothed combs that hecklers used to separate flax to make fibres for spinning. A list of what old occupations mean is at **www.scotsfamily.com/occupations.htm**.

Armed Forces: the Army

In ancient Scotland, men were summoned to arms, whether by the king, his feudal lords or the clan chiefs, by men running from settlement to settlement carrying a burning cross. The names of the men who responded to this call are not recorded. Similar militias were raised in the wars of the seventeenth century but for them NAS Exchequer series E100 contains 4,800 rolls, the earliest starting in 1641. These contain so many names that you can seldom be sure *an* 'Alexander MacGregor' is your 'Alexander MacGregor'. Later militia lists for the Napoleonic Wars can include useful details of payments to militia men's families: see the NAS Military Source List at **www.nas.gov.uk/guides/**.

C. Dalton's *The Scots Army, 1661–88* (repr. Greenhill Books, 1989) transcribed some rolls, the focus being mainly on officers. It includes officers' commissions found in State Papers: for 1688–1714 see Dalton's badly-named *English Army Lists and Commission Registers, 1661–1714* (Eyre & Spottiswoode, 1892–1904).

The yeomanry or volunteer corps could be raised by the justices of the peace in case of invasion, and from 1797, the Scottish Militia Act arranged for militias to be raised by a ballot of able-bodied men aged 18 and 45 (with some exceptions – those who did not want to serve could pay for someone else to go in their stead), except schoolmasters and men with more than two children aged under ten. Their records, in local archives, are best sought using A. Morrison's *Some Scottish sources on militias, fencibles and volunteers* (A. Morrison, 1996) and J. Gibson and M. Medlycott's *Militia Lists and Musters, 1757–1876* (FFHS, 1994). They are worth a shot if you are stuck, as the records (attestations) list age, occupation, and birth-parish, and sometimes include personal remarks. Wives of enlisted men sometimes applied for dependant allowances, giving children's names and ages.

From 1707, many Scotsmen served in Scottish regiments of the British Army. Army records are in TNA, Kew, in department WO (War Office). For sons of crofting or cottar families, joining the army meant escape from the tedium of subsistence farming and the tyranny of landlords, and provided a guaranteed pension and a chance to see the world. In the Napoleonic Wars of the late eighteenth century up to 1815, great numbers of young Scots were enlisted. In the Highlands, chiefs wishing to demonstrate their loyalty to the Crown went to great lengths to encourage their tenants to join up: the Duchess of Gordon went amongst her clansmen with six pipers, offering a guinea and a kiss to each recruit. The Countess of Sutherland pretty much ordered 500 young men from her tenantry to join the Sutherland Highlanders: they obeyed, little suspecting she would repay their loyalty with the Highland Clearances.

The specifically Highland regiments start with the Black Watch, created in 1739, followed by Loudoun's Highlanders in 1745, and Montgomery's (77th) and Fraser's (78th) Highland Regiments in 1757, and so on, officered by junior kinsmen and tacksmen of the chief. The idea was to drain potentially troublesome young warriors away from the Highlands, and harness their energies in Empire-building. After Culloden, the only Scots allowed to play bagpipes and wear tartan were those in the Highland regiments: ironically, as these were raised on a geographical basis, they thus preserved clan identities at the very time when the Government was trying to stamp them out. Numbers involved were substantial: 65,000 Scots were soldiers in 1763, mostly Highlanders. Between 1797 and 1837 Skye alone provided some 700 officers, 10,000 men and 120 pipers to the British Army, and half the farms there were rented by officers on half pay.

Besides the regular regiments, there were fencible (homeland defence) regiments of full-time volunteers raised by landowners between 1759 and 1799, some serving in Scotland or England but more often in Ireland (see **www.regiments.org**). Records are in J.M. Bulloch's *Territorial Soldiering in the North-East of Scotland during 1759–1814* (New Spalding Club, 1914).

The army took Scots all over the British Empire. When their service ended, many chose to remain where they were stationed. As regiments were often recruited in specific places, knowing a soldier-migrant's ancestors can help pinpoint their place of origin. Equally, ancestors who you know merely as farmers may have spent their youth in uniform, serving in Africa or India: local histories will indicate which local regiment(s) there were and a speculative search may reveal your forbear. Regimental museums are worth exploring: details can be found online and are listed in T. and S. Wise's *A Guide to Military Museums and Other Places of Military Interest* (Athena, 2001), and *Exploring Scottish History* (M. Cox, ed, Scottish Library Association, 1999): a visit to the National War Museum in Edinburgh Castle is also worthwhile. A good summary of the Highland regiments is in the back of F. Adam, *The Clans, Septs, and Regiments of the Scottish Highlands*, (1908, rev. edn, Sir T. Innes of Learney, 1970).

Officers: Until the twentieth century, officers – from generals down to second lieutenants – were almost entirely from the middle and upper classes. C. Dalton's *George the First's army 1714–27* (Eyre & Spottiswoode, two vols, 1910–12) covers the period to 1727. From 1740 there have been regular *Army Lists*, with basic details of all officers. TNA has much documentation on officers, the main being 'services of officers on the active list' in series WO 25 and 76, partially indexed, dating back to 1829 and in some cases to 1764,

including age and place of birth. Records of WW1 officers are indexed at
www.catalogue.nationalarchives.gov.uk.

Other ranks: Non-officers' service records from 1760 to 1854 are indexed
at **www.catalogue. nationalarchives.gov.uk**, through which the records
themselves can be sought. Because records are generally arranged by
regiment, it is best, for soldiers after 1854, to try to discover their regiment
from a mention elsewhere, such as the birth record of a child, or pension
records. Besides service records, you can also use muster rolls, pay lists – a
few of which go back to 1708 – description books (some back to 1754) and
records of casualty, desertion, attestation, discharge, prisoners of war and
pensions, which were paid through Chelsea (London).

Army births, marriages and deaths: Do bear these in mind: a family you
may have encountered as civilians may well have started with the marriage of
a soldier – anywhere in the world.

First and Second World War: many Other Ranks' service papers were
blown up, but some two million are still extant, so it's always worth searching
for an ancestor here. The many published memorials include the *National Roll
of the Great War 1914–18* (National Publishing Company, 14 vols, 1918–21),
containing information on about 150,000 men. All British Army First and
Second World War armed forces deaths are indexed by the GRO, London,
online at **www.findmypast.com**. Deaths, war graves and war memorials are
indexed by the Commonwealth War Graves Commission at **www.cwgc.org**.

Medal rolls: these tell you by implication the campaigns in which men
served, and are in TNA series WO 372. Those for the First World War,
partially substituting those service records that are lost, are online at
www.documentsonline. nationalarchives.gov.uk.

The Royal Air Force

This was formed in 1918 by amalgamating the Army's Royal Flying Corps and
the Navy's Royal Naval Air Service, founded in 1912 and 1914 respectively, all
with records in TNA. See W. Spencer, *Air Force Records for Family Historians*
(PRO, 2002) and the RAF Museum for more information.

Royal Marines

Established by Charles II in 1665 to serve as soldiers on navy ships, they fall into
three divisions: Chatham, Plymouth and Portsmouth. Records are in department
ADM at TNA, in whose Research Enquiries Room is a card index to most
attestation forms (ADM 157/1–659). See G. Thomas, *Records of Royal Marines* (PRO
Publications, 1994). Also useful is the Royal Marines Museum, Eastney Barracks,
Southsea, PO4 9PX, 0239 281 9385, **www.royalmarinesmuseum.co.uk**.

Royal Navy

For the seventeenth century, see J. Grant's *The Old Scots Navy 1689–1710*
(London, 1904) and the Admiralty Court records. From 1707, many Scotsmen

appear in the (British) Royal Navy's records at TNA in department ADM (Admiralty). See B. Pappalardo, *Tracing Your Naval Ancestors* (TNA, 2003) and N.A.M. Rodger, *Naval Records for Genealogists* (PRO Publications, third edn, 1998) and if possible visit the National Maritime Museum, London.

Officers: commissioned officers (from admiral down to lieutenant) between 1660 to 1845 are outlined in:

- J. Charnock, *Biographia Navalis, or impartial memoirs of the lives and characters of officers of the navy of Great Britain* (vols 1–4 and supplemental vols 1–2 by R. Faulder 1794–98).
- J. Marshall, *Royal Naval Biography* (Longman, Hurst, Rees, Orme & Brown, 1823–35).
- W.R. O'Byrne, *A Naval Biographical Dictionary* (John Murray, 1849, repr. 1861).
- *Navy Lists*, published from 1782.
- *The Naval Who's Who 1917*, covering many First World War officers.

Officers' service papers and other records are at TNA.

Ratings: until 1853, non-officers were only employed – sometimes against their will – per voyage, so can be very hard to locate in ships' musters: if you can't guess the ship, you may not find them. From 1853 to 1923 they appear in 'continuous service engagement books', fully indexed in ADM 188/245–7 and now indexed on **www.nationalarchives.gov.uk/**, which give dates and places of birth. Muster rolls in ADM 36–9 (1740–1808, with a few back to 1688) can lead you from ship to ship, and will tell you age and place of birth from 1764, together with other details such as tobacco and clothing allowances. Pay books, seamen's effects and papers, medal rolls, description books and pension records can also be consulted at TNA. Pensions were paid through the Chatham Chest (records from 1653–7 and 1675–1799) and then through the Royal Naval Hospital, Greenwich.

The Merchant Navy

The term 'merchant navy' covers all the British ships not in the Royal Navy. The best guide is C. and M. Watts, *My Ancestor was a Merchant Seaman* (third edn, SoG, 2004). Records are in TNA department BT (Board of Trade). There are some muster rolls from 1747, but most are from the mid-nineteenth century. Records are generally arranged by port, making them very hard to search except between 1835 and 1857, which are indexed in the 'registers of seamen', BT 120, 112, 119 and 114, leading straight to crew lists (BT 98), which give age and place of birth. BT 114 can also be used to look up 'seamen's tickets' (1845–53) which include date and place of birth. After 1857, searching reverts to being very hard, until 1913–41, which is covered by a Central Index Register of Seamen at TNA.

A great deal of merchant naval material, including many post-1861 crew lists, can now be found at the Maritime History Archive, Newfoundland, Canada (**www.mun.ca**), which offers an online search service. Those who died at sea between 1852 and 1889 are indexed in BT 154. Further records to search include ships' log books. Many boys and men were trained for the merchant navy by the Marine Society, whose indexed registers 1772–1950 are at the National Maritime Museum, Greenwich. Medals awarded to merchant seamen who served in the Second World War (some 100,000 of them) are now searchable online at **www.documentsonline.nationalarchives.gov.uk**.

From 1845 (and compulsorily from 1850), new merchant navy captains (masters) and second-in-commands (mates) could obtain a 'certificate of competency'. Including year and place of birth, the records are indexed in BT 127. Other records of them include a list covering 1868 to 1947, giving date and place of birth, in Lloyd's Marine Collection at Guildhall Library, London.

Between 1752 and 1796, bounties were paid to encourage 'buss fishing', which entailed catching herring using vessels with proper decks, weighing between 20 and 80 tons. E508/49/9–96/9 at the NAS contains records of the payments, listing the whole crew, their parish of birth, height and hair colour. Similar bounties for whaling 1750–1825 are in E508/47/8–130/8, with ship owners identified in E5021.

David Dobson's 'The Mariners of …' series, published in St Andrews in various volumes covering much of the Scottish coast, reports several sources' details of mariners such as:

'LOVE, John, master of the Happy Return of Greenock, 1710 (CTB.24.297)
LYAL, Robert, master of the brig Sisters of Greenock, 1786 (SRO.CE60.11.10)
MCALLISTER, John, skipper, son of John McAllister shoemaker, burges of Dunbarton, 1784 (DnBR).'

Coalminers

Many records of the old mining companies that were nationalized under the National Coal Board are in NAS class CB. These include some wages books and pay books (mainly twentieth century) and some records of company-run insurance schemes.

Customs and Excise

Ancestors involved with the sea may appear in Exchequer records of customs dues collected at ports, dating from the 1300s. Various accounts are in NAS E71–E74 (1498–1707). Collectors' quarterly accounts (E504, 1742–1830) list ships entering or leaving port, naming the master and owners.

Customs officers were also called 'tidewaiters', for they waited on the tides that brought in ships bearing taxable goods. Their reports are in NAS CE51–87, and mention many names of local people in the ports. If your ancestor was a customs officer, then more can be found on them in NAS class CE3 (catalogue) and CE12 (establishment books), both 1707–1829, and E502 (salaries).

Excise officers, including Robert Burns, collected dues and sought out those trying to evade paying them. Details of salaries are in NAS E502: also useful are J.F. Mitchell's notes on excisemen 1770–1830, on microfiche in the

NAS searchroom. Burns' own poem about excisemen tells us exactly what they were there to prevent:

> *'The De'li cam fiddling thro' the town,*
> *And danced awa wi' the Exciseman;*
> *And ilka wife cried 'Auld Mahoun,*
> *We wish you luck o' your prize, man'.*
>
> *We'll mak our maut, and brew our crink,*
> *We'll dance, and sign, and rejoice, man;*
> *And mony thanks to the muckle black De'il*
> *That danced awa wi' the Exciseman.'*

Doctors

In the Middle Ages, Scotland boasted a rabble of chirurgeons, apothecaries and barbers (who doubled, terrifyingly, as surgeons). Later medics who had studied the subject often appear in the university alumni lists, and those who were qualified can be sought in the records of: the Royal College of Physicians of Edinburgh (9 Queen Street, Edinburgh, **www.rcpe.ac.uk**), dating from 1681; the Royal College of Surgeons of Edinburgh (Nicolson Street, Edinburgh, EH8 9DW, **www.rcsed.ac.uk**), from 1505; and the Royal College of Physicians and Surgeons of Glasgow (234-42 St Vincent Street, Glasgow G2 5RJ, 0141 227 3234, **www.rcpsg.ac.uk**), from 1599. Many 'doctors' were very poorly qualified, some having attended a few series of lectures at university, or read a bit about the subject – but even this was not compulsory. Having said that, Scottish education produced many very good doctors, whose work was appreciated around the globe.

An excellent secondary source for doctors, dentists and midwives is P.J. and R.V. Wallis' *Eighteenth century medics (subscriptions, licenses, apprenticeships)*, part of the Project for Historical Geography Research Series (1994). Registration of medics started in 1858 with *The Medical Register*, which was then published annually, listing medics, with their address and qualifications (leading you back to the records of the professional bodies). There is also the *Medical Directory for Scotland 1852-60*, which became *The London and Provincial Medical Directory 1861-9*, then *The Medical Directory*.

There are similar annual lists of chemists (from 1869), dentists (1879), midwives (from 1917) and nurses (from 1921) in good libraries. Records of nurses 1885-1930 are in NAS HH2/33-7. If your ancestor was treated in hospital, there might be records of their treatment. These are best sought through **www.scan.org.uk** under the keywords 'health' and 'health boards'.

Freemasons

Freemasonry has dual roots, in groups searching for esoteric knowledge, and in lodges of working masons. By the eighteenth century, it had evolved into a form of Friendly Society whose main roles were social and charitable. Lodges proliferated in Scotland, and membership lists appear in Justice of the Peace records. Some lodge records are in archives, and most others are with the lodges, who are now reasonably well disposed towards researchers, but the records will often merely confirm that an ancestor was a freemason, and tell you no more, making them rather unrewarding as genealogical sources.

Government officials

An incomplete list of these, with salary and pension details, is in 'civil and judicial establishment 1707–1830' in the NAS Historical Search Room.

Industrial workers

As the 1700s and 1800s progressed, many people were drawn off the land and into the industrial towns, so that by the 1840s, almost a third of Scots no longer worked on the land.

Workers might change industry seasonally, labouring, say, as brickmakers in the summer and in the gasworks in the winter. Business records can be sought through **www.scan.org.uk** and through I. MacDougall, *Labour Records in Scotland* (Edinburgh, 1978), which should include Friendly Societies and other organizations aimed at mutual help. Factories treated their employees as day-labourers, so few records were kept: those that exist usually just give names, and perhaps how much was paid. However, if you have time and inclination, they may repay close examination.

Industrial accidents, especially those in the mines, were investigated by sheriff courts and reported in local newspapers. Those many industrial workers who fell on hard times may be chronicled in the records of poor relief.

Innkeepers

From 1756 onwards, anyone selling alcohol had to have a licence from the burgh, if they were in one, or else from the local justice of the peace.

Insane

Asylums and madhouses (and their records) generally date from the mid-nineteenth century, with records in the sheriff courts. From 1858, asylums were subject to the General Board of Commissioners in Lunacy, with records in NAS class MC. A 'Return of lunatics or idiots at large in the county of Edinburgh' for 1850 is in NAS AD58/114. Also worth searching if you suspect a history of insanity in the family (and, let's face it, who doesn't?) is NAS JC54/13–41, containing reports naming lunatic paupers throughout Scotland. Holders of heritable land who were considered insane had their rights exercised by curators, who were appointed in retours.

Jacobites

Some lists of rebels who fought on the Stuart side in the 1715 and 1745 rebellions, and in other rebellions such as the Duke of Argyll's in 1685, are in

Register of the Privy Council of Scotland, which is printed and indexed from 1545 to 1691, and names of some 1715 rebels are in the lists made by James Campbell of Stonefield, Sheriff Depute of Argyll, published in N. Maclean-Bristol's *Inhabitants of the Inner Isles, Morvern and Ardnamurchan, 1716* (SRS, 1998). The 1745 rising is better documented. A. Livingstone, C. Aikman and B. Hart (eds)'s *No Quarter Given – The Muster roll of Prince Charles Edward Stuart's army 1745-6* (Aberdeen University Press, 1984) and B. Seton and J. Arnot (eds)'s *Prisoners of the '45* (SHS, 1928-9) are worth searching. In 2008 the Culloden visitor centre **www.nts.org.uk/ Culloden/PPF/Legacy** invited children descended from participants in both sides of that battle to send in their family trees.

Literati

The John Murray Archive **www.nls.uk/jma/ index.html** has over 150,000 items concerning people involved in 'literature, science, politics, travel and exploration' between 1768 and 1920.

Members of Parliament

All known members of the Scottish Parliament to 1707 are in M.D. Young's *The Parliaments of Scotland* (Edinburgh, 1992). From 1707, Scottish MPs at the House of Commons, Westminster, London, are included in *The History of Parliament*, Wedgwood House, 15 Woburn Square, London, WC1H 0NS, 0207 862 8800, **www.irinfo.ac.uk/hop/** , which currently covers MPs from 1386 to 1832 and Members of the House of Lords from 1660 to 1832.

Motorcar owners

Some local archives hold details of early car registration. Dundee Archives's records for Perthshire (1909-11) and Kinross-shire (1904-52) are online at **www.fdca.org.uk/ registrations.htm**. For example:
'*527 Mrs. Caroline F. Drummond Forbes, Millearne, Auchterarder, 14 hp Siddeley Side entrance Phaeton body, painted blue with white lines, [weight unladen] 19 cwt, [use] Private, [registered] 17 April 1909, [notes] Trans[ferred]. 23 Feb. 1911 to David Morgan Graham, Pitreuchie, Forfar. (Mar. 5 1912)*'.

Railwaymen

Scotland's many private nineteenth-century railway companies' records contain varying degrees of information about their staff (drivers, plate-layers, station masters and so on), though virtually nothing for unskilled employees and the navvies who originally built the lines. NAS BR/RCH(S)/5 will help you guess, by location, which company may have employed your railway ancestors, and company records can then be sought in NAS class BR. For more help see T. Richards' *Was Your Grandfather a Railwayman?* (FFHS, 1989) and the NAS guide on **www.nas.gov.uk/guides/**.

Postmen

Post Office Establishment books date back to 1803 and are in NAS PO1/15-65 up to 1911, detailing staff in main Post Offices, including letter carriers, though not sub-postmasters, but many of these were listed in directories.

Schools and Universities

Thanks to the Church of Scotland, all children aged five and upwards received basic education from the seventeenth century onwards, though poor children could seldom afford to remain after eight, unless helped by bursaries.

There were no school holidays, but most children were let off to help their families during harvest time. Besides religious instruction, the schoolmaster (or *dominie*) taught reading and writing, with some Latin for older children, and only in the burghs did arithmetic feature strongly on the curriculum. All this contributed enormously towards forming the 'serious-minded' Scottish character that made Lowland Scots natural leaders in the cultural enlightenment of the 1740s and the Industrial Revolution, bringing untold (and often unsung) benefits to Britain as a whole.

The *dominie* was appointed and paid by the kirk sessions or by the burgh. Burgh records contain records of hiring and firing: my probable relative John Paterson was sacked from his job as schoolmaster of Selkirk in July 1613, accused by the Minister of being '*insufficient both for reading, and teaching, and the counsel not liking him, he had been given warning at Candlemas*'. In the countryside, kirk sessions, the records of the heritors and local presbytery that confirmed the *dominie*'s appointment can be equally informative. Schoolmasters often doubled-up as kirk session clerks and later as census enumerators and registrars (for whose conduct see NAS GRO1). From 1847, your schoolmaster ancestor may have belonged to the Educational Institute of Scotland (see NAS GD342), and if he was a schoolmaster in Aberdeenshire, Banffshire and Morayshire from 1832 you can see if they received assistance from the James Dick Bequest Trust, in NAS GD1/4.

Secession churches often had their own schools and schoolmasters, detailed in their own records, and Catholic schools appeared after the 1829 *Catholic Emancipation Act*. In addition to parish schools, you may find 'adventure schools', set up by private teachers who '[ad]ventured' their own money in the projects.

Scotland had some orphanages (called hospitals) funded by charitable endowments, particularly George Heriot's School, Edinburgh (NAS, GD421), Dean Orphanage (GD 417), Dr Guthrie's Schools (GD425) and the Orphan Hospital (GD417). Their records can give names, ages and some information on the children's backgrounds. The *Statistical Accounts* usually refer to schools existing at the time.

State-run mass education was introduced to Scotland in 1872, taking schools away from church control and placing them under new school boards. Whilst in England similar legislation brought education to the masses for the first time, in Scotland, in most cases, 1872 simply saw a small administrative change in an on-going system. The boards' records are divided between local archives and the NAS.

The Society in Scotland for Propagating Christian Knowledge (SSPCK) worked from 1709 to establish church schools to help eradicate 'popery and ignorance' in the Highlands and Islands. NAS GD95 records its schoolmasters and school inspections: see also A.S. Cowper (ed), *SSPCK Schoolmasters, 1709–1872* (SRS, 1997).

From 1872 schools kept logbooks, some of which are now kept in local archives, not in the school. At best, though, the logbook will simply be a mere list of names. More interesting are leaving certificates ('highers'), listing each candidate's subjects, grades and marks, in NAS ED36 (arranged by parish), available from 1906 but closed for 75 years. In ED52, for fun, you can see reports on individual schools' meals from 1946.

Fee-paying schools generally keep detailed records of pupils, sometimes including ages and fathers' names. Some of these are published, such as those for Edinburgh Academy, Fettes College and Loretto School, and most also produced rolls of honour commemorating ex-pupils who died in the World Wars.

Scotland's education system produced many potential university students. The oldest universities are St Andrews (1410); Glasgow (1451); Kings College, Aberdeen (1495); Marischal College, Aberdeen (1593); and Edinburgh (1582). Records of graduates of all but Edinburgh are published; the amount of genealogical information (ages, fathers' names and so on) varies. Many Scots also studied beyond Scotland, at Oxford and Cambridge, but more often in the Protestant universities in northern Europe.

The burghs

If your ancestors were amongst the small proportion of Scots who lived in towns or cities, you may well be able to trace them through records that are not available for people living elsewhere. The records make burgh-dwellers rather interesting and desirable ancestors to have.

There were four types of burgh or merchant settlement. The main and most numerous were royal burghs, with charters from the Crown, created from the twelfth century onwards. Sometimes, they were created out of nothing, as a means of 'civilizing' an area, and in others the status, with its accompanying trade rights, was granted to existing settlements. By 1707, there were 66 of them, ranging from cities to tiny villages. In addition there were burghs of regality, which also had Crown charters; burghs of barony, which were imitations of royal burghs and had charters granted by the local laird; and, from 1833 onwards, there were police burghs, with police forces and other municipal responsibilities.

Seventeenth-century Scotland had no large cities: Edinburgh in the 1650s had a mere 30,000 inhabitants, so crowded into narrow wynds and tenements that it took less than half an hour to walk the city end-to-end. Glasgow, Dundee and Aberdeen had less than 10,000 souls a-piece, and most burghs were vastly smaller. The relative safety and sophistication of burgh life was marred by terrible sanitation, most inhabitants emptying chamber pots from their windows, or using loos that jutted out over the wynds, with terrible consequences for passers by below. In Edinburgh, by 1773, the practice of flinging effluent from windows had been forbidden, but, introducing Dr Johnson to the city that year, Boswell was still embarrassed at 'his being assailed by the evening effluvia' of the city. Not surprisingly, burghs were rife with rats, fleas, lice and diseases such as typhus and summer diarrhoea.

The smallest burghs were little more than hamlets, dominated by the local laird and populated by peasant burghesses, who only practised crafts once they had attended to their fields and animals. Kilmaurs, Ayrshire, for example, was a burgh of barony, with a charter from the Earl of Glencairn, whose proud burghesses spent their time growing and selling kale.

The burghs were largely self-governing, with the right to elect baillies (similar to magistrates), run a merchant guild and maybe also craft guilds. Royal burghs could elect MPs and send commissioners to conventions of royal burghs. The greatest privileges of the burgh were trading rights over their hinterlands (or 'liberties'), some of which covered entire counties. In addition, until 1672, royal burghs had a virtual monopoly on foreign trade.

Burgesses

Freemen of the burgh, known as burgesses or burgers, were divided into merchants and craftsmen.

Merchants. The members of the burgh's merchant guild dominated the burghs. Merchants spent a lot of time preserving their exclusive rights to foreign trade from the craftsmen below them by keeping control of the town council. Few merchants specialized in specific commodities: most bought shares in whatever ventures were afoot, usually shares of ships and their cargoes, and then prayed hard that they arrived safely. These shares are recorded in shipping registers, some of which are in NAS class CE and others are in burgh archives.

Trade brought merchants wealth, sometimes equal to that of the highest nobles. As land brought status (and, one should imagine, some fresh air) there were many transitions from merchant to laird, either by purchase of an estate or by marriage to a laird's heiress. Consequently, most burghs were surrounded by a ring of estates owned by merchants.

Most burghs were dominated by small cliques of merchant families. Seventeenth-century Dundee, for example, was dominated by the Goodmans, Haliburtons, Wedderburns and Clayhills.

Craftsmen ranked below the merchants. They included tailzers (tailors), blacksmiths, skinners, saddlers, cordiners (cordwainers or shoemakers), weavers, goldsmiths and armourmakers. In some burghs, from about 1450 onwards, craftsmen formed craft guilds to prevent competition from non-burgesses tradesmen rather than as any guarantee of quality: indeed, because they had to produce cheap goods for sale in the countryside, Scottish craftsmen had a reputation abroad for being rather shoddy. Their records may include pension records and payments for funerals.

Craft guilds could be very small: in 1604, Glasgow had a mere 361 guild members, only five in the dyers' guild and only two in the surgeons' guild. The barrier between merchant and craftsman was usually impenetrable: only in seventeenth-century Glasgow did the rules give craftsmen equal footing with merchants, a measure of egalitarianism that helped the city's great commercial success.

Becoming a burgess: this could be done by patrimony (being the son of a burgess), marriage (marrying the daughter of one), apprenticeship (being apprenticed to a burgess), or redemption (paying for admission). The latter could be an expensive business: in 1600, it cost £67 for a stranger to become a burgess of Edinburgh.

Incomers took several forms, including younger sons of landed families who were not due to inherit land, and also sons of indwellers whose fathers made enough money for them to be apprenticed.

Apprentices (whether sons of outsiders or burgesses) were usually boys aged between 14 and 21, bound to their masters, upon payment of a fee by their families, for five to seven years. Having finished the apprenticeship, one became a journeymen, paid by the day (the word comes from the French for day, *journée*), and might go on to submit an 'assay' or 'master piece' to become a burgess and (if not a merchant) a master craftsman. Those wishing to join a guild (merchant or craft) had then to trade for four years, two of them unaided by a servant or apprentice, or else pay a fine, or, best of all, marry your master's (or another master's) daughter. Those who completed the course were often denoted 'B. & G.B.', 'Burgess and Guild Brother', and were eligible to stand for office within the guild, such as that of the deacon.

Using the records

Burgh records usually include their own registers of deeds and sasines, town council minutes and the records of the trade and craft guilds. The records are scattered between NAS (class B), university libraries and burgh archives: look on www.scan.org.uk, or ask the relevant burgh archivist. Printed material will be identified in D. and W. Stevenson, *Scottish Texts and Calendars* (SHS, 1987).

Burgess often had voting rights, so will be shown in poll books, which listed voters and said how they voted. Available in local archives, these are useful for indicating when people were alive and for identifying different people of the same surname in the burgh.

Some apprentice indentures are in burgh deeds registers, and others are in NAS RH9/17/274-326. Those on which tax were paid in the period 1710-74 are indexed by the SoG (searchable on **www.britishorigins.net**), and some have been published (such as records of Edinburgh apprentices 1583–1800, published by the SRS). They often give the father's name and trade, and some, such as those of the Incorporation of Gardeners of Glasgow, might cite a 'craft genealogy' going back several generations.

The great emphasis on family continuity within burghs makes their records valuable genealogical tools. Records of apprenticeship, or admission as a burgess by patrimony or matrimony, usually provide the father's name, and the latter of course reveals links to the wife's father as well. You can often trace a web of interconnected families through these records. Matrimony was a popular system because, by marrying his daughter to an up-and-coming burgess, the father ensured a comfortable retirement for himself, whilst the son-in-law gained the experience, social contacts and financial backing of an established family. The result could be seen as a form of matrilineal succession – reminiscent, coincidentally, of ancient Pictish society – whereby you can sometimes trace back several generations most easily through the female line.

Non-burgesses

Indwellers (or 'inhabitants') were the 'unfree', non-burgess residents of burghs. They paid their taxes but had no say in how the place was run. Most were poor (and were kept so by the system), such as journeymen, servants, carters, night-soil carriers and prostitutes. The well-off, such as nobles and notaries, were often made honorary burgesses.

There were plenty of craftsmen living outside the burghs who had no connection to guilds (though the indentures of the few who were apprenticed may appear in registers of deeds). Some belonged to mutual benefit societies (see MacDougal's *Labour Records in Scotland*), and occasionally they appear in oral history. In 1695, Martin Martin reported a smith in Kilmartin, Skye, who could cure 'faintness of the spirits' by laying people on his anvil and then threatening them with his hammer: he was apparently the thirteenth generation of his family of smiths able to exercise this curious power.

Landholders

Generally, those who held land were better recorded than those who did not, because the acts of buying, inheriting and holding land entailed the creation of records. This makes them useful ancestors to have. Their records can also shed light onto those who occupied their lands.

The upper echelons of the landholding system comprised royalty, and below them were the nobles: dukes, marquises, earls, viscounts and barons. After them came the knights and baronets and then the lairds, whose hereditary titles were tied to the land. All such people usually had coats of arms, and were described as 'of' somewhere, such as 'James Matheson *of* Dougaltoun' (those described as 'in', i.e. 'James Matheson *in* Dougaltoun', were not land holders). The landowning class included most clan chiefs, some of whom were granted titles.

Original records for tracing landowners are generally quite detailed, though also somewhat redundant as so many of their pedigrees have already been traced and recorded. These are the best places to start looking:

- Margaret Stuart, *Scottish Family History* (1930, repr. GPC 1994).
- Joan P.S. Ferguson (ed), *Scottish Family Histories* (NLS, 1986), which updates and enlarges on Stuart.
- NLS catalogue **www.nls.uk**.
- Catalogue of printed works in the SoG **www.sog.org.uk**.
- Catalogue of the Royal Historical Society **www.rhs.ac.uk/bibl/bibwel.asp**.

For the peerage, see also:

- James Balfour Paul (ed), *Scots Peerage* (Edinburgh, 1904–14).
- *Burke's Peerage, Baronetage and Knightage*, published in 107 editions since 1826. The 107th (2003) publication, edited by Charles Mosley, includes the pedigrees of the clan chiefs even if they never received peerages. It is also available online at a subscription website, **www.burkes-peerage.net**. Burke's also published many editions of the *Landed Gentry of Great Britain and Ireland*, that includes numerous non-titled Scottish families.
- The holdings of the Scottish National Portrait Gallery.
- *The Dictionary of National Biography* and its modern re-write *The Oxford Dictionary of National Biography*.
- P. Bell's *Who Was Who in Edwardian Scotland* (Edinburgh, 1986), which indexes ten illustrated county biographical dictionaries covering about 2,000 prominent people.
- Lord Lyon's records.
- Manuscript (i.e. unpublished) sources for landholders include the NAS's collection of genealogies in RH16, the collections of individual family papers in NAS class GD (Gifts and Deposits), and the John McGregor Collection of genealogies and genealogical notes on mainly Highland families, particularly Campbells and MacGregors, in GD50.

Grants of land

The holding, gaining and inheritance of land (or heritable property) generated a great many genealogically useful records. The system was a feudal one, instituted by the Canmore kings, and consequently its terminology – retours, inquests, clare constat, tailzies, *beneficium inventarii*, *ultimus haeres* – is drawn variously from Scots, Latin and Norman French, so can be rather terrifying for the uninitiated. In most cases, however, the jargon merely describes people inheriting or buying land.

Remember that some fairly small farmers and tradesmen held land, and (as is often suggested by their surnames) a huge number of poor families are descended from younger sons of landholders.

Since 1964, unless a will says otherwise, Scottish estates are divided equally amongst the heirs. Before 1964, unless a will said otherwise, primogeniture, the exclusive succession of the eldest son, applied. Before 1868, wills could not affect the inheritance of land, so the eldest son always inherited. If there were no sons, the daughters inherited equal portions as heirs portioners, and if there were no children, the next eldest brother inherited (if the deceased had older and younger brothers, the younger ones inherited before the elder ones). If no brothers, the sisters became heirs portioners. Once someone has died, the person due to inherit becomes the 'apparent heir', until they 'complete the title', i.e. complete the process of inheriting the land.

Under the Canmore kings' system the Crown assumed ownership of all of Scotland and became the 'superior'. By Crown charters, the Crown then *feud* or granted land, either in perpetuity to institutions such as universities or burghs, or to individuals or vassals as heritable property. Recipients of such charters were 'subject superiors'. They could hold the land themselves or sub-infeudate it, by further charters, to their own vassals or tenants.

Crown charters, granting land to subject superiors, appear in the records of the Great Seal, Privy Seal, and Signatures (drafts commissioning a charter). Abstracts from the *Registers of the Great Seal of Scotland* (RMS or *Registrum Magni Sigilli Regum Scotorum*) have been published from its start, 1314, up to 1668 (in Latin to 1651). They are indexed for people and places. The abstracts contain much genealogically useful information, and provide reference numbers to the original documents, which are in NAS class C. The period 1668–1919 is covered by typescript indexes to the grantees and lands in the three categories of original records (the Register of the Great Seal, Paper Register and Principality Register). 'Signatures' were written in Scots and, although drafts, often give the salient details: names, lands and date. They are in NAS SIG1–2, 1607–1847.

The 'reddendo' section of a charter includes details of the 'duty of feu', i.e. what the vassal must pay or do in return for the land. In the Middle Ages land was usually held by *blanche ferme*, in return for occasional payments, or by ward holding, in return for military service. By the late sixteenth century, most holdings had been converted to *feu ferme*, by which land was held in return for a regular rent of produce or, more commonly, money. Usually, conditions included several sorts of 'casualties' or special payments: ward casualties were paid by minors until they reached 21; casualties of marriage were paid until the heir married; casualty of non-entry was paid between the death of the vassal and the entry of his heir to the land, and when he did he paid a casualty of relief.

Charters were also granted by subject superiors to their own vassals. They are usually mentioned in relevant sasines. The records were not registered publicly, so will only be in archives in deposits of family papers. Those in the NAS are, for this reason, indexed in RH6, 1142–1600. Other sources for charters include RH9/15, containing writs of land for Shetland and Orkney, and Miscellaneous Charters and Writs in RH6-8, which must be searched manually. Charters granted by the Lords of the Isles appear, with annotations, in J. and R.W. Munro's *Acts of the Lords of the Isles* (SHS vol. 22, 1986).

Inheriting land

The inheritance of land by subjects superior was controlled by services of heirs, also called retours, or precepts of clare constat. In theory, one could only be given sasine of heritable land once one of these processes had been completed.

Retours or services of heirs: these are records of inheritance of land held by subject superiors, i.e. held direct from the Crown. Because they are covered by detailed indexes, it is sometimes possible to trace a line of landowners back using services to heirs alone.

The process started with the heir approaching Chancery. A brieve (or writ) of Chancery would be issued, instructing the sheriff or burgh court to establish, by inquest, who was indeed the true heir. The records (or 'repertories') of those courts may contain details of the inquest, including sworn testimony from witnesses (those for Jedburgh sheriff court are published as *Services of Heirs, Roxburghshire 1636–1847* (SRS vol. 69). The verdict, if positive, was then returned or 'retoured' to Chancery, who consequently allowed the heir to inherit the land by being given sasine of it. Retours came in several forms, including general retours, whereby the heir was acknowledged generally (by general service), and special retours, whereby someone was acknowledged as the heir to specific pieces of land (special service).

The retours were recorded in Chancery, starting in 1530. They are in Latin (except for the Commonwealth period, 1652–9), up to 1847. Summaries of the retours up to 1700 are published in *Inquisitionum Retornatarum Abbreviatio* (full title *Inquisitionum ad Capellam Regis Retornatarum Abbreviatio*). The period 1544–1699 is also covered by a SGS CD. Both are indexed for people and places. From 1700 to 1859 there are indexes for each ten years, and from 1860 to the present there are annual indexes. They are available on SGS CD for the period 1700–1859. The printed and CD versions usually give all salient information about a case, but if you want to explore further you can use the references given in the indexes to order up the original documents in the NAS.

If you don't find what you want, remember some retours between 1303 and 1622 were omitted from the foregoing, but are transcribed in C39/4. Some slightly pre-1700 retours actually appear in the post-1700 records. For 1700–1846 some retours, omitted from the indexes, appear as a supplement to the 1905–6 volume.

Royal burghs and some franchise courts, such as Dunfermline and Dunkeld, issued their own services of heirs. These are not included in the Chancery records, and appear in the records of those burghs and courts instead.

The retour process was also used to appoint guardians for children whose fathers had died. Retours tutory appointed tutors for pupils (boys under 14 and girls under 12) and retours curatory appointed curators for children from those ages up to 21, and also for the mad.

Unfortunately, not all heirs completed the process as soon as their predecessor died. Some waited years or even decades or just occupied the land regardless. In some cases, fathers granted land to their eldest son while they were still living, by deed, to avoid the hassle. But even when a retour is missing, though, there may be a sasine anyway.

Clare constat: the right of sub-tenants to inherit land was acknowledged by the subject superior by what was called a precept of clare constat. These did not have to be registered, but might be referred to in subsequent sasines, or in family muniments (such as those in NAS class GD, 'gifts and deposits'). If found, they can be valuable because they tend to recite an heir's descent from the ancestor to whom the land was granted originally. If the process proved complicated or contentious, a precept of clare constat could be taken to Chancery (the Lord Chancellor's court) and may appear in the services of heirs.

Tailzies

From 1685, landowners could control what happened to their land by a deed of tailzie (the Scots' equivalent of the English 'entail'). These are sometimes referred to in a service of heirs. A tailzie might prevent heirs selling off land, ensure succession by those who would not normally be the legal heirs (such as illegitimate children), or force sons-in-law or maternal grandsons due to inherit family land to adopt the surname of the original owner.

The register of tailzies (NAS RT1) begins in 1688. It is indexed 1688–1833 in the Historical Search Room, and then (in the Legal Search Room) by a manuscript index 'Register of Entails' (RT3/1/1–2) that runs from 1688 again right up to 1938. Tailzies could only be broken from 1848 onwards, and these disentails also appear in the registers.

Sasines

Sasine is the Scots word for the act of giving or investing people with entitlement to land, and happened whenever land changed hands. This was often when land was inherited, but vassals of any sort could alienate (sell), wadset (mortgage) or assign (by a marriage contract, for example) their holdings to someone else during their lifetime, provided they had consent of the superior from whom the land was held.

Sasines and their phraseology seem daunting to the uninitiated: 'giving sasine', 'instruments of sasine', 'taking of instruments', becoming 'seised in', 'infeft in', or given 'sasine of' land all mean basically the same thing. The arcane nature of the terminology (rather like that of heraldry) is because, although it is used now of paper records, it arose to describe physical objects and actions. In ancient times, and right into the Middle Ages, ownership of land was signified by being handed a rock or clod of earth from the land concerned. The Scots understood this practice well, for when the ships of the Milesians first approached Ireland at the end of their voyage from Spain, their ancestor Heremon, son of Milesius, is said to have severed his own hand and thrown it ashore, so that he could claim possession by having touched it first – an act commemorated to this day by the Red Hand of Ulster.

Less dramatically, sasine came to be given by handing over a symbolic piece of earth, and later by written documentation alone. Up to 1660, sasines were recorded by notaries, though few survive out of the many that must have existed: those surviving for royal burghs are in burgh archives or in the NAS (class B). The NAS holdings for those outside burghs are in NAS class NP. The NAS catalogue and D. and W. Stevenson, *Scottish Texts and Calendars* (SHS, 1987) will show you what has been published.

Notaries were not averse to taking bribes to make up sasines that never existed, or lose ones that did, so in 1599 the State established the Secretary's Register, which ran until 1609, as a more reliable and secure place for recording sasines. Its records are now incorporated into the two registers that succeeded it, from 1617: the General and Particular Registers of Sasines. These are all in NAS class RS.

The Particular Register was divided into counties (hence its being 'particular'): pages 77–8 of the NAS guide relates particular registers to modern counties and states whether they are indexed up to 1780 (only nine out of 40 are not) and if so for what periods, and whether indexes have been published (24 out of 40 have). Particular Registers that have not been indexed are best searched using the minute books, or, failing these, searching through the register itself.

The General Register should also be searched. It is indexed to 1735. The period 1736–80 can be searched using the minute books, in NAS RH62.

From 1781 onwards, there are printed abridgements of sasines, covering the Particular and General Registers (the latter was abandoned in 1868). These have now been digitized and are fully indexed up to the present, by place (except between 1831 and 1871) and person. The abridgements usually provide all the information given in the original document, but the originals can be ordered and studied if desired. Some registers of sasines have been microfilmed by the Mormons.

The General and Particular Registers do not include sasine registers in royal burghs until the twentieth century. Up till then they are in the burgh registers, with the earliest recorded in Dysart in 1602. The records are generally in Scots. Some are indexed: all this is indicated by the NAS catalogue (look up the name of the burgh under class B). Those for Glasgow are at Glasgow City Archives, Aberdeen's pre-1809 are at Aberdeen City Archives and Dundee's pre-1890 are at City of Dundee Archive and Record Centre.

Valuation rolls

Kept from 1643 onwards, these were an aid to taxing people on the land they owned or occupied. They are useful for learning about landowners, whose estate records can then be sought. They sometimes provide direct information on tenants, but generally don't mention sub-tenants.

They are due to be searchable on ScotlandsPeople by 2010. For 1643–1854, they are in exchequer records (NAS E106), arranged by county. L.R. Timperley's *A Directory of Landownership in Scotland c.1770* (SRS, 1976) is based on the 1771 rolls, and is indexed. Various rolls for the 1810s to 1850s are in IRS4 (and identifiable using the NAS catalogue). Some turn up in heritors' records too. The records do not cover royal burghs, though for Dunbar, Inverkeithing, Jedburgh, Linlithgow, North Berwick and Peebles before 1855 there are rough equivalents, the cess or stent rolls, in NAS class B.

For 1855 to 1988 they are more inclusive, omitting only tenants paying less than £4 per year. There are annual valuation rolls covering each county and burgh, detailing each piece of land and buildings, stating who owned and occupied them (naming heads of households). These are divided between NAS class VR and local archives. Some include place name or street indexes, as identified in the catalogue, though even with these aids they will be slow to search. They are useful for pinning down when people came and went from homes between the decennial censuses.

Heraldry

The visible symbol of the landed class was heraldry. Heraldry is not confined to the rich: the younger sons of younger sons (etc.) of heraldic lords or clan chiefs were entitled to use arms, but those who were poor simply didn't have the means to display their arms, or perhaps didn't have any great interest in doing so.

Heraldry was introduced to Scotland by the Canmore kings and their Norman followers. It was then a very new idea, for whilst the concept of painting devices on shields and flags is as old as warfare itself, it was only in the twelfth century that the Normans and French started passing *the same* designs down from father to son, with younger sons and their descendants later 'differencing' the arms they had inherited by a small mark of cadence or, more commonly in Scotland, by a distinctive bordure placed around the original design.

Besides simply identifying knights on the battlefield, coats of arms became a way of identifying the male lines of families.

Scottish heraldry is regulated, very strictly, by Lord Lyon King of Arms and his heralds, who operate from offices in New Register House. Lyons have been appointed since at least the fourteenth century, and their office incorporates the much more ancient duties of the Gaelic royal sennachies, who were responsible for reciting the genealogies of the kings. Early Lords Lyon were concerned chiefly with ceremonial matters, and also granted and recorded the use of coats of arms, by authority of the king. The first proper record of Scottish heraldry was the armorial compiled by Sir David Lindsay of the Mount in about 1542.

The use of heraldry is controlled by strict rules, but they are easily broken, and by the seventeenth century the need to regulate the use of arms became pressing. In 1662 an Act of Parliament complained of younger branches of families assuming the arms of their senior cousins without differencing their arms, and '*other mean persones, who can nowayes derive their succession from the families whose names they bear*' assuming those same families' arms anyway. In 1672, Lord Lyon established a proper 'Public Register of all Arms and Bearings in Scotland', which is still maintained today. Details of all arms granted and/or registered to people (and also to institutions such as burghs, universities and companies) up to 1902 are published in Sir J. Balfour Paul's *An ordinary of arms contained in the public register of all arms and bearings in Scotland* (William Green and Sons, second edn 1903), with an additional volume published in 1977 covering upto the 1970s.

Lord Lyon's office is a treasure-house of the genealogies of families entitled to use arms, the best of which have been updated regularly since the seventeenth century. The 'Public Register of Genealogies' contains two types of record: birthbrieves, which record, where possible, all 16 great-great-grandparents, and linear pedigrees which aim to trace the male line as far back as possible. Early entries tend to be terse (maybe just names and no dates), becoming sometimes over-detailed in the eighteenth and nineteenth centuries, including copious notes, for example, of the military achievements, awards and decorations of Napoleonic War officers. The records are at the ScotlandsPeople Centre and on **www.scotlandpeople.gov.uk**.

The main rules are simple: don't bear arms undifferenced if you are not the senior representative of the family, and don't bear arms at all if you have not been granted them yourself, or are not descended *in the male line* from someone who had been – and where heraldry is concerned, male-line descent must be proved with 100 per cent, watertight documentary evidence.

In any event, do nothing without having your evidence examined and approved by Lord Lyon. These lions, I am delighted to report, have teeth in the form of extensive powers of criminal jurisdiction: they fine people who misuse heraldry, and seize and destroy artefacts displaying unauthorized arms, sometimes at great cost to their owners.

This is not such an elitist field as you may think: Thomas Innes of Learney calculated in the 1950s that one in every 45 Scots was entitled to bear arms. Lord Lyon does not permit anyone with a 'clan' surname to use 'clan arms' (which are strictly those of the chief and his proven kin alone), but the clan crest can be used by clansmen and clanswomen who, in Lyon Court's words, '*... are the Chief's relatives, including his own immediate family and even his eldest son, and all members of the extended family called the "Clan", whether bearing the Clan surname or that of one of its septs; that is all those who profess allegiance to that Chief and wish to demonstrate their association with the Clan.*'

It is correct for these people to wear their Chief's Crest encircled with a strap and buckle bearing their Chief's Motto or Slogan. The strap and buckle is the sign of the clansman, and he demonstrates his membership of his Chief's Clan by wearing his Chief's Crest within it.'

Estate papers

Landholders' estate records are important not just for studying landowning families, but also for learning about their tenants or tacksmen and, to a much lesser extent, their tacksmen's sub-tenants. Published estate records (such as many of the Sutherland estate papers that have been published by the SHS) are listed in D. and W. Stevenson, *Scottish Texts and Calendars* (SHS, 1987). Original records are in the NLS, local archives and private hands, and NAS class GD (Gifts and Deposits), with others in RH (especially 9, 11 and 15) and CR (Crown Estate papers for Glenlivet and Fochabers). These can be searched in the NAS catalogue under the appropriate reference (GD, etc.) and the relevant family name.

Some are disappointing, but others, such as the 1814 records for Blair Drummond Moss, Kincardine, Perthshire, 1814, name everyone in each family. Another splendidly detailed survey is John Hume's *Survey of Assynt*.

The Forfeited Estate Papers concern estates confiscated from landholders who supported the Stuart risings. They are in NAS E601-63 for 1715, E700-88 for 1745 (look in the NAS catalogue under these references and the name of the estate). The estates were administered by factors appointed by the Commissioners of the Annexed Estates and the records can include occupants of the land, rentals, claims, and details of how the estates were improved prior to being sold off.

Tacksmen and tenancies

The Scots for 'lease' is *tack*, and the larger takers or lessees of land were called tacksmen, sometimes described as occupiers or possessors. Tacksmen form a rural 'middle class' between the landowners and their own sub-tenants, the small farmers and cottars.

Many leases were regularly renewed, enabling families of tacksmen to stay put for centuries. Boswell reminds us that *'the tacksmen or principal tenants, are named by their farms, as Kingsburgh, Corrichatachin; and their wives are called the mistress of Kingsburgh, the mistress of Corrichatachin …'* The historian John Prebble adds, *'these tacksman took titles from the land they leased, were mac-This of That or The Other, and were as sensitive as sea-anemones on matters that touched their honour.'*

Tacks may be found in registers of deeds, and will tell you a little about the tacksman, what he leased, and how much rent he paid. Some records of them, and the resulting rentals and surveys, survive in the records of the landowner (see under estate papers). Sadly, though, most tacks were never registered: when the tack expired, it was thrown away. Luckily, court records are full of disputes over tacks, especially due to non-payment of rents and consequent evictions.

Dr Johnson wrote that the tacksman was 'commonly a collateral relation of landowner', for landholders generally granted tacks to close relatives, so as to guarantee a good supply of fighting men in times of trouble – the tacksmen were the officers whilst their sub-tenants were the foot soldiers. After the battle of Culloden, the system began to break down, and Johnson tells us that by 1773 *'the ancient dependent is in danger of giving way to a higher bidder, at the expense of domestick dignity and hereditary power'*. But as late as 1785, an English traveller complained:

'The chieftan lets out his land in large lots to inferior branches of his family, all of whom must support the dignity of lairds. The renters let the land out in small parcels from year to year to the lower class of people, and to support their dignity squeeze everything out of them they can possibly get, leaving only a bare subsistence. Until this evil is obviated Scotland can never improve.'

For us, however, the system provides valuable clues for working out likely relationships. Whilst you cannot be dogmatic about what the relationship 'would have been', you can be pretty confident, in the absence of any other evidence, that if X MacKie was the tacksman and Y MacKie was the laird, then X and Y were pretty closely connected by blood.

In the same fashion, and for the same reason of breeding up loyal fighting men, tacksmen tended to sublet their land to their own kin, as discussed later.

Farmers and crofters

Most Scottish ancestors were not landholders, so were described as 'in', not 'of', the place where they lived. Unfortunately, their tenure of land was often informal, providing little security for them and few written records for us. However, even if you cannot trace them back generation by generation, you can still learn a lot about the sort of people they were by studying their social history.

Farmers

Up to 1700, virtually all (80–90 per cent) of Scotland's million or so people lived on the land, evenly scattered between bog and mountain. Roads were virtually non-existent and the meandering tracks linking the settlements were generally impassable, save on foot or horseback: the fact that people say carts *could* travel between Glasgow and Edinburgh in good weather speaks volumes for the situation over the rest of the country.

Arable land was hard to come by, so large villages were rare. Most Scots lived in small hamlets, maybe a dozen or so per parish. Hamlets were called bailies in the Highlands, and farmtouns in the Lowlands (or kirktouns or clachans if they had a church, milltouns if there was a mill, or cottouns if they supported only cottars).

The tacksmen who leased land generally farmed only part of it themselves and sub-tenanted the rest to small farmers, who did most of the work of actually cultivating the soil and tending the animals. Just as tacksmen were often relatives of their superior, so too might the tacksman's tenants be his own kin. Unfortunately, the difference between knowing this as a general fact and proving it in your particular case may be enormous, the problem being the lack of written records. Sub-tenancies were usually verbal arrangements, and estate papers that list the sub-tenants are very rare.

Cottars and labourers

Below the farmers came the great mass of cottars, also called pendiclers or grassmen. They are sometimes confusingly termed 'landless': in fact, they held land, totally informally, but only a hut with space for a kale-yard or potato patch, and no grazing rights for a cow. Cottars might pay their rent to the tacksman, but were more often under-tenants of the small farmers. In the Highlands, you even find cottars on parts of crofts – not living in a shoe like old Mother Hubbard, but crouched, so-to-speak, in the shoe's toe. They grew what little food their patch would allow, and tried to earn money elsewhere, serving or labouring for those above them, following them into battle when required, and – despite their poverty – as deeply attached to the land as everyone else. Cottars were not always hard-up, for some worked as tradesmen, such as blacksmiths, shoemakers, weavers, carters and potters. In times of poor harvest, they might actually be happier than small farmers, though their conditions never even approached those of their counterparts in the burghs.

Life for eighteenth-century Ayrshire cottars was immortalized in Burns' 'The Cottar's Saturday Night', in which:

'The toil-worn Cotter frae his labour goes,
This night his weekly moil is at an end,
Collects his spades, his mattocks, and his hoes,
Hoping the morn in ease and rest to spend,
And weary, o'er the moor, his course does hameward bend.'

We learn much about his home, his prayers and his way of life, including what his children are doing:

'Belyve, the elder bairns come drapping in,
At service out, amang the farmers roun';
Some ca' the pleugh, some herd, some tentie rin
A cannie errand to a neibor town:
Their eldest hope, their Jenny, woman-grown,
In youthfu' bloom-love sparkling in her e'e–
Comes hame, perhaps to shew a braw new gown,
Or deposite her sair-won penny-fee,
To help her parents dear, if they in hardship be.'

In the Lowlands, from the 1700s onwards, there was a tendency to consolidate smallholdings into bigger farms. Many families were uprooted, and became hinds (landless labourers), hired at the local feeing fair on six-month or year-long contracts, living with their families in chaumers (lofts over stables), a corner of the farmhouse itself, or in bothies (wooden huts) – the latter being somewhat notorious for the bawdy songs and sexual freedom engendered by their primitive conditions. Some hinds, especially in the Lothians, might be hired on the same farm on a rolling basis all their lives, but the itinerancy of the less fortunate is often reflected in census returns that show each child in the family being born in a different parish. Hinds often had to supply a female servant or bondager, usually their wife, daughter or sister. Many made the transition to industrial labourers, or fell the short distance down to the bottom of the pile as vagabonds and beggars – often from families that, a couple of generations before, had known their laird as their kinsman.

Besides the OPRs, cottars and hinds may appear in kirk sessions or local court records, and usually the poorer, drunker, randier and more dishonest your ancestors were, the better the chance you'll have of finding them, sometimes with a genealogical detail such as an age or place of birth. Less exciting mentions may include court records of witnesses or General Assembly lists of heads of households, especially those petitioning for the appointment of this minister or that. The kirk sessions may list people in communion rolls; 'mortifications' recording bequests of money for charity and the poor people on whom it was spent; labourers hired to mend roads, bridges and church buildings; and the sadly rare 'testificates' that recorded where incomers had been born.

The Poor

The term 'poor' was reserved for those in need of outside help. The 'undeserving poor' comprised vagabonds, drunks and 'ne'er-do-wells', whom Knox condemned as '*stubborn and idle beggars who, running from place to place, make a craft of their begging*'. The 'deserving poor' were '*the widow and fatherless, the aged, impotent and lamed*', or simply hard-working families faced with starvation through bad harvests or unemployment. From the 1690s, the deserving poor were the responsibility of the parish, specifically of the kirk sessions and heritors (see below). A caveat in the system was that, to receive relief in the parish, you had to have been born there, or gained right of settlement by marrying a local man or by having lived there for seven years without causing trouble.

The 1845 *Poor Law Act* established parochial boards, independent of the church, in each parish (which became, for that purpose, civil parishes). The transition took a few years, so kirk session and heritors' records are still worth searching a few years after 1845. In 1894, responsibility was transferred again, to local councils. The boards' minute books and accounts (which are closed from the 1930s onwards) can provide varying degrees of detail about applicants and what relief they were given, but most useful are their Registers of the Poor. Surviving records are generally held in local archives, and can be sought through **www.scan.org.uk**, and some are in NAS class CO. Registers of the Poor can include name, age, marital status, religion, occupation, name, age and income of spouse, and details of children, siblings and parents. They will say why the application was being made and, crucially, where people were born – particularly useful when seeking famine migrants from Ireland.

Registers of the Poor do not survive for Edinburgh, Dundee City or Aberdeen, but the Glasgow area is superbly well covered, specifically for Glasgow (from 1851), Barony (1861) and Govan (1876), and for other local parishes in Bute, Dunbartonshire, Lanarkshire and Renfrewshire, to 1948. They are at Glasgow's Mitchell Library (North Street, Glasgow, G3 7DN, 0141 287 2999, **www.mitchelllibrary.org**), indexed to 1900. Some other areas' records are online, such as those for Liff and Benvie Parochial Board 1854–65 and Dundee East's poorhouse register (1856–78), at **www.fdca.org.uk**. For more, see K.M. Forbes and H.J. Urquhart's 'Records in the National Archives of Scotland relating to Poor Relief, 1845–1930', *Scottish Archives*, 8, 2002, pp. 9–32.

Crofting

Crofting was a type of landholding peculiar to the Highlands and Islands, defined by the 1883–4 Napier Commission as holding land for agriculture or pastoral purposes individually or in common (perhaps by runrig), direct from the proprietor, at a rent of up to £30 a year. (The same commission defined cottars as occupying homes without agricultural land, worth up to £2.) The system started in the eighteenth century, when some lairds cut out the tacksmen and started renting land directly to small farmers, allocating each a parcel of the former farm as a croft.

In theory, as long as the rent was paid, the croft passed down from father to son (thus encouraging families to make more effort to look after their land than they had when they knew they might be moved on if the tacksman lost his lease). An exception was the early-nineteenth-century system (called *suidhicheadh*) of allocating crofts for seven years and then rotating the families.

Sometimes, as families grew too big, crofts might be subdivided or parts would be sub-sub-let as homes for cottars (who might often be poor relatives of the crofter, or the previous croft-holder who, for whatever reason, had been unable to keep up the rent).

Kelp

A further motivation for landowners to introduce crofting was the kelp industry. Soda ash (sodium carbonate), made in southern Europe by burning certain plants, especially barilla, was used in many British manufacturing processes, such as glass and soap. The French Revolutionary and Napoleonic Wars (1793–1815) cut Britain off from these supplies, but it was found that the kelp that grew copiously around the Highlands and Islands had similar properties to barilla. As demand soared, so did prices, and lairds encouraged their tenantry to engage in the filthy work of growing, collecting and burning kelp. Some lairds cleared people to live on the coast in crofts deliberately designed to be too small to sustain families through agriculture alone.

On Harris, for example, the relatively fertile west coast is now largely deserted, due to families being cleared away in the 1790s, whilst the inhospitable, rocky east coast is peppered with crofts built for kelp farmers.

Despite the horrible nature of the work, kelpers flourished, and their tiny crofts became full of relatively healthy, happy children. Then, in 1815, the Napoleonic Wars ended, cheaper Continental minerals flooded back in, the kelp price plummeted and the crofters' incomes evaporated. Worse, they were now stuck on coastal crofts that could not sustain them. As if that wasn't enough, farmers used to collect kelp as fertilizer for their fields, but during the boom they had preferred to burn it for minerals. Consequently, the fields of 1815 were far less fertile than they had been in 1793.

The end of the wars also opened the seas to commercial shipping that offered passage to the colonies. Driven from the land by the collapse of the kelp industry, many people sailed abroad. Those who clung on then had to face the Potato Blight of the 1840s and 1850s, and a further wave of emigration ensued. Many descendants of the crofting families of Harris now live in Cape Breton, Canada.

The Clearances

Until a few decades ago, the Highland Clearances were seldom talked about. Descendants of people who had been cleared knew little or nothing of what had happened, and cared less. In 1963, Penguin Books published John Prebble's *The Highland Clearances*, and awareness of the events of the late eighteenth and early nineteenth century came back into sharp focus.

Only a small number of clans took part in the '45, but in the government backlash that followed, all clans lost the right to bear arms, to wear tartans and kilts, and for their chiefs to exercise hereditary jurisdiction. The clan system started to crumble.

As government-imposed law and order spread north, the need to sow dragon's teeth – to use your land to raise fighting men – became redundant. Settling in Edinburgh, chiefs quickly forgot their ancient obligations to their kinsmen, and became absentee landowners. Within a generation of the battle of Culloden, few young chiefs spoke Gaelic, many married Lowland wives, and their desire for ready cash soared. Their land was seen simply as a source of revenue, no more. The administrators of the Confiscated Estates of 1745 had shown how lands could be 'improved' by abolishing runrig, bringing in Lowland farmers to replace native tacksmen, and consolidating land into large farms, on which were reared black cattle that could be sold for beef.

Cattle cannot graze everywhere, so for a few decades the pace of change in the Highlands remained only moderate. But it was soon realized that the right sort of sheep could survive practically anywhere. As war with France loomed, the price of meat rose sharply and Highland lairds looked greedily at the profits that could come by replacing their distant kindred with the new, profitable 'four-footed clansmen'. Encouraged by progressive agriculturalists like 'Agricultural' Sir John Sinclair of Ulbster, the lairds brought hardy Cheviot sheep across the Cromarty Firth in 1790, and in 1792 they reached Caithness. '*Mo thruaighe ort a thir*,' cried a seer in the Highland townships, '*tha'n caoraich mhor a' teachd!*' – '*Woe to thee, oh land, the Great Sheep is coming!*' Merchants, half-pay officers and Lowland farmers started offering good money for tracts of Highland land that previously had been considered worthless – provided, of course, the existing small farmers were removed. The Highland Clearances had begun in earnest.

As tacks came up for renewal, they were terminated, and when the tacksman was removed his sub-tenants had no rights at all. Small farmers, crofters and cottars could simply be told to leave their holdings, and go they must. Occasionally, 'warning away notices' were issued by the sheriff courts, but usually no paper trail exists. Sometimes people were actively encouraged to emigrate, though usually they were offered alternative holdings on the least desirable land, often by the sea where fishing and (until 1815) kelp farming meant they could still be profitable to the estate.

1792 is remembered as *Blaidhna nan Caorach*, the Year of the Sheep, when tenants in Ross-shire tried driving the sheep back south. They were met by the local yeomanry and three companies of the Black Watch, summoned for fear that the protestors were Jacobites. Thereafter there was little resistance, for everyone knew the Government would support the lairds and their sheep before people.

It's hard to take sides now on the basis of surname or clan loyalty. Within the MacLeod clan, for example, many tacksmen, sub-tenants and cottars named MacLeod were cleared from their ancestral lands, yet MacLeods were amongst the soldiers who enforced the process. A scion of the Chiefs of Assynt, Donald MacLeod of Geanies (1745–1834), was the sheriff depute of Ross and Cromarty who brought in soldiers in the *Blaidhna nan Caorach* to defeat the tenantry.

The greatest landowner in the northern Highlands, so by default the worst offender in the Clearances, was Elizabeth, Countess of Sutherland (1765–1839), *Ban mhorair Chataibh* or 'the great lady of Sutherland', wife of Lord Stafford, who later became Duke of Sutherland. James Loch, her chief commissioner, implemented a ruthless clearance policy with an army of factors and local commissioners. Between 1810 and 1812, they had cleared most of Assynt, Golspie, Loth, Clyne, Rogart and Dornoch. Prebble wrote that: '*The first white wave of Cheviot sheep broke over the Assynt hills before the people there had time to obey the writs of eviction. To the sound of phrenetic bleating, they pulled down their house timbers and walked with them to the coast where the villages in which they were to live had not been built, the boats from which they were expected to fish had not been launched, the nets unspun.*'

Prebble benefited much from the work of Donald MacLeod, a stone mason from Strathnaver, Sutherlandshire, who lived through these dreadful times and later wrote *History of Destitution in Sutherlandshire* (1841) and *Gloomy Memories in the Highlands of Scotland* (1857). '*A large portion of the people of these parishes*', wrote MacLeod, '*were in the course of two or three years, almost entirely rooted out, and those few who took miserable allotments ... and some of their descendants continue to exist on them in great poverty.*'

As time passed, clearances became yet crueller. The year 1813 was remembered as *Bliadhna an Losgaidh*, the Year of the Burnings. Until then, people had been allowed to take away their roof timbers, for wood was a scarce commodity in the Highlands. In 1813, fearing the disobedient people might return to rebuild their homes, factors started burning down farms, timbers and all.

In many cases, the year's crops were left to rot in the ground – or to be munched by the incoming sheep. We hear of desperate people creeping back in the winter to scratch for potatoes in the frozen fields, terrified of being caught trespassing. Donald MacLeod wrote that: '*Every imaginable means short of the sword or the musket was put in requisition to drive the natives away, or force them to exchange their farms and comfortable habitations, erected by themselves or their forefathers, for inhospitable rocks on the sea-shore ...*'

Nobody knows what numbers were involved. Between 1810 and 1820, between 5,000 and 15,000 people were evicted in Sutherland alone. Many of those who stayed were given coastal crofts and encouraged to fish, and harvest kelp. Of life on the coast, Prebble tells us that the coastal strips 'were narrow patches on the cliff's edge, or bordered by bog and morass.' The arable soil so thin that Donald Macleod wrote: '*In many places the spots the poor people endeavoured to cultivate were so steep that while one was delving, another had to hold up the soil with his hands lest it roll into the sea.*'

Seed was blown away, salt and mildew ruined the crops, and cattle trespassed inland, resulting in fines that the crofters could not pay for want of anything to sell. Needless to say, the occasional poaching of a sheep was punishable with transportation.

The Napier Commission

Highland families are a hardy lot. Despite the Clearances, the collapse of the kelp industry and the potato blight, a core population of survivors remained in their ancient lands beyond the mid-nineteenth century. But conditions remained pretty dire, and by the 1870s pressures for social reform were mounting – for by now, rural Scots were not an ignorant peasantry, but the products of church schools, very well aware of what was right and wrong, and, more to the point, what was decent. The 1870s and early 1880s saw the outbreaks of civil disobedience such as the Bernera Riot of 1874 on Lewis, and the Battle of the Braes on Skye in 1882, both protests against landlords taking away grazing rights because they wanted the land for game.

The crofters' plight concerned Gladstone's Liberal government. In 1883, he established a royal commission chaired by Lord Napier and usually referred to as the Napier Commission. During 1883, the commissioners travelled through the Highlands and Islands interviewing 775 crofters to discover exactly how they lived and what their grievances were. Transcripts of these interviews are published in the *Report of Her Majesty's Commissioners of Inquiry Into the Condition of the Crofters and Cottars in the Highlands and Islands of Scotland* (1884). A very readable analysis of the findings appears in A.D. Cameron, *Go Listen to the Crofters: the Napier Commission and Crofting a century ago* (Acair, 1986, repr. 2005), including a useful list of where and when the hearings were held.

The Napier Commission also sent forms to each estate owner requiring them to fill in details of their crofters and cottars:

- the name of each holder (but not the names of everyone else in the family).
- number of families in each croft.
- number of houses on the croft.
- total number of people living on the croft.
- rent and other dues such as labour that the tenants had to give in return.
- area of arable land.
- area of pasture.
- souming or summing, which was the number of horses, cows, calves and sheep they were allowed to keep: and also the number they actually had.
- the cottars' return asked for names, if their house was on someone else's croft, if they paid rent and if so to whom and what their occupations were.

The forms (save those for the Orkneys and Shetlands, which were lost) are in NAS AF 50 7/1–7/19 (crofters) and 8/1–8/7 (cottars), arranged by county and then alphabetically by estate: they are rather cumbersome to search, but worth the effort.

In the mid-nineteenth century, many crofters clung to the hope that a son enlisting in the 93rd (Sutherland) Highlanders guaranteed that his father's croft would still be there when he returned. John Sutherland of Musie in Rogart, Sutherland, told the Napier Commission:

'As an inducement to my father to enlist in the 93rd Highlanders, my grandfather got a promise of being left undisturbed in his lot during his lifetime, and if his son survived his term of service, he would succeed him. My father joined that regiment and was wounded at New Orleans. On the expiry of his service in the army he returned home and expected to succeed his father as tenant of the whole lot but, to make room for another man who was evicted from a sheep farm, my father was summonsed and deprived of the best part of his father's lot.'

Alexander MacCaskill, cottar and boatman in Soay said:

'My grandfather went to the army – at least he was forced to go – and his bones are bleaching on a West Indian island and now his grandson (myself) was evicted to a rock or island not fit to be inhabited.'

Nobody liked having to perform labour as part of their rent. John MacCaskill, cottar and shoemaker in Fernilea, Bracadale, Skye, claimed that in spring, summer and harvest he had to labour on the laird's land for up to three days a week at one shilling a day, time he should have spent (at much greater profit) making shoes. Alexander Cameron, cottar in Cuilmore, Skye, said that as part of his rent he had to provide a maid servant for the sheep farm at Drynoch for 50 days a year. His sister had filled this role, but then she married and, having nobody else to do the job, he was first threatened with eviction and then his rent was raised. Charles Cameron, crofter in Acharacle, Ardnamurchan, Argyll, said his rents were so high that his daughter working in England had to send money back: 'What she is able to give me helps to pay my rent and to support me.'

The people's demands were reasonable. They had all heard about the 'Three Fs' that underpinned Gladstone's 1881 *Irish Land Act* – Fair rents, Fixity of tenure and Free sale (freedom to sell their holdings, or otherwise be compensated for improvements they had made, if they gave their holdings up). They were aggrieved that the best land was devoted to sheep and deer, while they had to make do with the worst.

Gladstone could do nothing about the latter: to this very day crofts remain on poor land, while the rich shoot deer on the most fertile stretches. But he gave them rights, under the Crofters Act of 25 June 1886, allowing crofter and cottar alike the 'Three Fs', so that holdings could be passed down in the family, with a Crofters' Commission to adjudicate on fair rents. Some court cases brought by crofters from 1886 onwards, and by small farming tenants from 1912, can be found in the Scottish Land Court (NAS class LC), which is arranged by county, and indexed (the records are closed for 75 years).

CHAPTER 9

Clans and tartans

Many Scottish families belong to clans, and many more believe they are associated with one on the basis of a family surname. With the new surge in interest in family history, clans have been reinvented as societies with a strong emphasis on genealogy.

The clan system

Rather like black holes that can bend space, the clan system had an oddly warping effect on Scottish genealogy and continues to exert a force on Scottish family history that is absent from the genealogies of most other European countries. The main advantage it gives us is that, before the mid-eighteenth century, surnames can usually be localized to very specific areas and connected back to specific traditions and founders. The main disadvantages are that the system encouraged people to adopt surnames that were not theirs, and that once a surname is associated with a clan, many people believe that all bearers of the surname must, ergo, be members of that clan.

The earliest references to clans come from the 1100s (the earliest, apparently, is to the Clanna Morgan of Buchan), though that probably tells us more about the lack of earlier records than what was actually going on. The term simply means 'children' or 'family', and the idea derived from the ancient tribal system of the Picts, broken down and modified by the Dalriadan and Viking invasions.

By the time it emerges into recorded history, 'the clan' denoted a family, or mixture of local families who, regardless of their actual ancestry, professed a common descent from the clan's founder. They owed allegiance to a chief who was the living representative of the founder, whom they regarded as their senior kinsman. Clans often had several prominent branches, whose kinship was assumed, though could seldom be proved.

During what Dr Johnson called 'the ages of tumult and rapine', violence underpinned the clan system. The economy, such as it was, was based on farming black cattle, and raiding those of neighbouring clans. Raids led to blood feuds and vendettas, with blackmail and demands for 'protection money' thrown in. The famous Glencoe massacre of 1692, when the MacDonalds of Glencoe were massacred by Campbell soldiers to whom they were giving hospitality, was merely one in a web of inter-clan conflicts (the MacDonalds had once killed 100 Campbells by barricading them into a barn near Oban and setting it ablaze). To call his clansmen to arms, the chief would send runners through the region, bearing a blazing or fire-blackened cross. The men would gather and march to war. Actual violence was perhaps less prevalent than posturing, and we know that even blood feuds could be terminated by simple satisfaction of honour: compensation might be paid and signed guarantees would put an end to the vendetta.

Chiefs and clansmen

Chiefs were chosen by their close male-line relationship to previous chiefs. Under the ancient Gaelic system, the new chief could be a son or male-line grandson or great-grandson (or great-great: the limit varied) of any previous chief, chosen on the basis of his ability to lead the clan in battle (under 'tanistry', the chief could nominate his successor). By the 1500s, though, most clans had adopted primogeniture, whereby the eldest son succeeded his father. Great chiefs often had lesser ones to serve them: the Clan Rankin's chiefs were pipers to the MacLeans of Col, and the MacCrimmons served the MacLeods of Skye in the same way, with a piping school at Borreraig near Dunvegan. Johnson described the chief as '*the father of the clan, and his tenants commonly bore his name*'. His power was absolute: '*He told them to whom they should be friends or enemies, what King they should obey, and what religion they should profess.*'

Membership of the clan involved an obligation to fight and a consequent access to land. Genealogy was key to clansmen's belief in their membership of the clan, through which they derived their obligations and privileges. Their precise genealogical connection to the chief determined their hierarchy and precedence, and decided how land was allocated and indeed how they sub-allocated their holdings to their own minor kin. As W.H. Skene wrote in 1891, '*In such a state of society the pedigree occupied the same position as the title deed in the feudal system, and the sennachies were as much the custodians of the rights of families as the mere panegyrists of the clan.*'

Clan lands

The clan's link to land was tremendously important, but was never set in stone. The idea that clansmen had inalienable rights to their ancient lands is nonsense. Clan chiefs themselves had no compunction about moving clansmen about: in 1599, when Macdonald of Islay ordered his people to leave Kintyre, they went meekly (his actions pale into insignificance compared to MacLeod of Dunvegan who, in 1739, actually sold some of his people as indentured servants in the Carolinas, America).

As the tribal system became incorporated into the feudal system, many clan chiefs, those 'rugged proprietors of the rocks', as Dr Johnson called them, received Crown charters, or charters from their feudal superiors, for their lands. As Prebble puts it, '*The land was his [the chief's], its ownership long since settled by the swing of a broadsword, and although most chiefs had realized that paper now carried more weight in law than steel, their tribal or feudal levies still protected their title deeds.*' Some chiefs missed out, though, and found their land being granted to others. By 1590, several clans, such as the Camerons, Macnabs and Macgregors were landless, tenants of other feudal lords, many of whom were chiefs of other clans. Loyalty, however, remained with the chief, not the landlord. Smout quotes the example of the Earl of Huntly calling his tenants to arms in 1562. Amongst them were many MacIntoshes, but as Huntly's quarrel was not a MacIntosh one, the MacIntosh chief ordered his clansmen to return home – and home they went.

Highland and Lowland

The clan system refers primarily to the Highlands, but not exclusively so. Border clans are first mentioned in 1587, but had existed throughout the Lowlands in all but name for much longer. As the Crown weakened from the late 1200s onwards, Highland practices started spreading into Lowland dynasties, whose Norman or French nobles began to behave increasingly like their Gaelic neighbours. Even Robert II's son Alexander Stewart, Earl of Buchan (d. 1394 or 1406) called out his feudal host as if it was a clan, and led fearsome raids on his neighbours, earning himself the nickname, 'the Wolf of Badenoch'. One means of consolidating local power was by bonds of manrent, of which about 800 survive, mainly for the sixteenth century, whereby men bound themselves to their feudal superior in the reasonable expectation that they would be granted land as a result. The main tools, however, were tacks or leases granted by Lowland lords, like the Grants and Frasers, to 'gentlemen' of the lord's name, that created networks of patronage so akin to the clan system that this is what, effectively, they became. Smout writes that: *'economically, such "gentlemen" might be little more than peasants, but if they were the kin of the lord they had a family right to protection. When a great family rose to power, his surname rose with him: the rise of the Earls of Huntly in the north-east was accompanied by the rise of all the cadet branches of the family and by the proliferation of small tenants named Gordon throughout the counties of Aberdeen and Banff; when the cathedral of Dunblane fell into the hands of successive bishops surnamed Chisholm, its main offices were also held for generations by clerics surnamed Chisholm.'* The kinsman, he continues, *'gave earls and barons of his kin all the deep respect due by a son to a father, though he never treated them with the abject deference due from a mere commoner to a remote and mighty lord. The whole atmosphere of kinship was a complex one, compounded both of egalitarian and of patriarchal features, full of respect for birth while being free from humility. It appeared uncouth beyond Scotland mainly because it was a legacy of Celtic* [i.e. Gaelic] *influence unfamiliar to the outside world.'*

Smout summarized the situation by saying that the difference between Highlands and Lowlands was mainly one of emphasis: Highland clans were based on kinship modified by feudalism and Lowland families were feudal, tempered by kinship: 'Both systems were aristocratic, unconscious of class, designed for war.'

The end of the clan system

The clan system started to unravel in the early eighteenth century due to forfeiture of land after the 1715 rebellion. Yet it still functioned until the

'45, when clan loyalties were a major factor determining the choosing of sides.

Dr Johnson writes of the situation before Culloden: the clansmen were *'perhaps not unhappy … a muddy mixture of pride and ignorance, an indifference for pleasures which they did not know, a blind veneration for their chiefs and a strong conviction of their own importance,'* while the chiefs themselves *'walked out attended by ten or twelve followers, with their arms rattling.'* In *The Sea Kingdoms* (HarperCollins, 2001), Alastair Moffat repeats a story told to him in Skye that 'appears in no written version' of the battle of Culloden: as they stood in the sleeting rain, waiting for battle, some of Charlie's men sang the twentieth Psalm, but others recited their genealogy so that *'while the government soldiers were shouting abuse and challenges … the clansmen were remembering why they had come to fight. For their families, for their history and the land from which neither was divisible'*. In the next few hours, many of them were laid low by Redcoat grapeshot.

Seeing how easily Bonnie Prince Charlie had been able to call out the clans, the state took vigorous steps to wipe them away, ending the chiefs' powers and banning the wearing of tartan.

The clan chiefs played a large part in dismantling the system themselves when they began to look for ways to make the land yield greater profit. When they stopped seeing their clansmen as beloved kinsmen the stage was set for the Highland Clearances. *'The estate perhaps is improved,'* said Johnson, *'but the clan is broken.'*

Tartan

Tartan could easily have become a curiosity consigned to museums and history books. Instead, it has been reinvented as a symbol of the Scottish nation, whether Highland or Lowland.

Tartans started off as patterns common to particular Highland districts or settlements. As these areas also happened to have dominant ruling clans, the district's distinctive tartan became associated with these too, becoming specifically *clan* tartan. The patterns have evolved considerably since then, so some now may bear little resemblance to those used in the past.

Tartan was not found outside the Highlands until the Act of Union in 1707 that formally united Scotland with England, when, according to Sir Walter Scott, Lowlanders started wearing it in protest against the English, paving the way for it to become a symbol of Scottish identity. Calling the clansmen to arms in 1745, Prince Charlie draped himself in Royal Stewart tartan, creating a direct link between tartan and Jacobitism. Consequently, tartan was banned in the aftermath of the '45, and the law was not repealed until 1782. When tartans reappeared, they may or may not have been the same as those worn before 1745. The first published source for tartan is the *Vestiarium Scoticum*, first produced in the early 1800s by the Allen brothers, who claimed to be grandsons of Bonnie Prince Charlie (they weren't). Their book purported to contain descriptions of the distinctive tartans of the clans of sixteenth-century Scotland,

and, forgery or not, it cemented tartans into the heart of Scottish national consciousness. After this came a rash of publications listing district, family, clan, clergy, Highland, Lowland and general tartans, up to 600 in all.

Tartans are recorded at Lord Lyon's Office (**www.tartanregister.gov.uk**). Whilst anyone can sell any type of tartan, registered or made up, it is a criminal offence to sell a registered tartan labelled as something it is not, or which represents a registered one inaccurately. As new ones are discovered or invented and accepted, the number registered increases. As Charles MacKinnon of Dunakin put it, *'Tartans and Highland dress are today regarded as the emblems not of the Highlands alone but of all Scotland. When we find Smith tartan being advertised, as we do now, it is clear that the great band of Scottish Smiths have joined the ranks of those who claim to be "entitled" to a tartan of their own. Why not? They were never a clan, but if Kidds and Coburgs can have their tartans, why not Smiths?'*

Clan badges

It seems likely that, before the eighteenth century, plant badges, not tartans, were the main means of telling clansmen apart. Each clan had one: heather for the MacDonalds, fir for Grant and holly for MacIntosh. A list of badges is in F. Adams' *The Clans, Septs and Regiments of the Scottish Highlands* (National Library of Canada, 1965). Each has a story attached to it. The Morrions, for example, use pieces of driftwood. They were hereditary brieves (judges) under the Lordship of the Isles, but fell into relative obscurity after the seventeenth century. Their Gaelic name is Mhic Gille Mhoire, 'sons of the servants of St Mary', but their traditional descent is from Mores the son of Kennanus, an illegitimate son of the King of Norway who, with his wife and child, was cast ashore on Lewis clutching a piece of driftwood.

The genealogical implications of the clan system

Modern guides to Scots families, such as *Collins' Guide to Scots Kith and Kin* (1953), list many septs or divisions under Clan names. These septs were created for several different reasons: for example, the Clan Chattan's Smiths are descendants of Henry Gow, a Perth smith who once stood in for a missing member of Clan Chattan in a fight against the Clan Kay in 1396. The Beatons, one of 18 surnames listed under MacLeod of Harris (and Skye), were probably originally Bethunes from Flanders, established in Angus by the twelfth century and then at Balfour, Fife. A Beaton of Balfour became a physician and settled in Skye, passing his skills on to his descendants there, and as physicians to the MacLeods, they became regarded as a sept of the MacLeods. On the other hand, the Griers are a sept of the MacGregors because of direct descent from a son of the eleventh MacGregor laird.

Clearly, of the world's millions of Smiths, only the descendants of Henry Gow are part of Clan Chattan. The only Beatons who belong to the Clan MacLeod are the descendants of the physician. Only the Griers who are descended from the eleventh MacGregor laird are part of Clan MacGregor. So, if you're a Smith, a

<table><tr><td rowspan="10">More tartans</td></tr></table>

- Scottish Tartans Authority, Fraser House, 25 Commissioner Street, Crieff, Perthshire PH7 3AY (0)1764 655444 **www.tartansauthority.com**
- Sir Thomas Innes of Learney's *Tartans of the Clans and Families of Scotland* (Edinburgh, 1938; eighth edn, Johnston & Bacon, 1971)

Beaton or a Grier, it's not your surname alone but this plus your family tree that will show whether you are part of one of the Clans Chattan, MacLeod or MacGregor. In the absence of a proven pedigree, the best you can do is see where your direct line lived as far back as you can trace them: if this was in the area occupied by these septs, then you may indeed be a member.

Far more worrying for we genealogists is the statement, found in many books on clans, that people who wanted clan protection simply adopted the surname of the local clan and, by inference, ditched their original surname. This would imply that farmer Black one day saw laird MacDonald, riding over the hill, and declared, 'I'm a MacDonald, of proud MacDonald blood, and you're my distant kinsman!' But that is nonsense, of course: in a culture underpinned by genealogical knowledge, no such imposture would ever be believed and the local sennachie would have had Black for breakfast.

People may well have adopted clan surnames that were not originally their own, but where oral history survives, so too will the knowledge that there was not a blood link. In my own experience of oral village history, people often know which people of their surname aren't related. In his *Harris in History and Legend* (Birlin, 2002, 2006), a modern sennachie, Bill Lawson, cites an example from Harris where a change was remembered. At the end of the eighteenth century a young boy called MacDonald on the estate of Captain MacLeod was such a good poacher that, when the captain was unable to find deer to hunt, the boy still led him to a herd. The captain rewarded the boy with land to build a house, and bade him call himself MacLeod, which he and his descendants continue to do – but still knowing their original identity.

It's only once such oral knowledge has gone that mistaken beliefs about kinship based on surnames arise.

Bill Lawson's wife Chris told me of a grey area – where oral knowledge was fading, but not gone completely. She has three lines of ancestors now surnamed MacLeod, but who, in their own oral tradition, were called Bànaich ('the fair people'), Glasaich ('the grey people') and Clann 'ic Leòid. The latter definitely considered themselves to be true MacLeods, though without any supporting genealogical evidence. The Glasaich and Bànaich, she thinks, may have been given the surname MacLeod by the minister or estate clerk, simply because they had no proper surname, but lived in a predominantly MacLeod area. However, nobody can know for sure that they didn't have an earlier tradition of MacLeod ancestry.

Sometimes, lines of clansmen can be traced back to clan chiefs. Bill Lawson told me a story from Tarbert, Harris, of Norman MacLeod of Tarbert (c.1756–1846), whose son Alexander settled in the Philippines and wrote a letter to his aunt Mary MacLeod in Cape Breton, on 14 June 1895. He signed himself: *'Alasdair mac Thormoid mhic Neill mhic Thormoid mhic Thormoid mhic Iain mhic Neill. Am bheil an t-sloinntireachd? (is that pedigree correct?)'*

Another descendant of the same family, now in Skye, recited the same pedigree and told Bill that the earliest Neil was 'Niall a chaidh a'chrochadh ann a Lit' – Neil who was hanged at Leith. Bill thinks it likely that this was Neill MacLeod, who was hanged there in 1613 (the number of generations works).

This Neil embodied the most characteristic qualities of his clan. His indictment reads:

'From your very youth you being trained up in all manner of barbarous cruelty and wickedness, and following the pernicious example of your godless parents, kinsfolk and country people, having committed innumerable oppressions, heirschipes and violent deeds … ye accompanied Norman McClaud, your brother, with two hundred barbarous, bloody, and wicked Hielandmen … in warlike array, with bows, darlochs, two-handed swords, hag-butts, pistols and other weapons … sentenced to be hanged at the Market Cross in Edinburgh, his head planted on a stake and his lands forfeited.'

Neil, says the indictment, was one of the illegitimate sons of Roderick, last chief of the MacLeods of Lewis. Thus, the MacLeods, descendants of Norman of Tarbet, can be traced back to the MacLeod chiefs of Lewis.

Sadly, many families just cannot make firm links like this. Between your earliest known ancestor and the chiefs of their name there may simply be untold generations who were not recorded, and you cannot know if the male line had always had the surname, or had adopted it. DNA offers hope for many, because genetic tests are proving that many people with clan surnames share the same Y-chromosome DNA, proving a male-line connection with each other.

The MacLeods in Badnaban furnish an example of how a tentative link might be found using some oral history and surviving population lists.

MacLeods in Badnaban

Before the Assynt OPRs start in 1798, few families can be traced back with certainty, but Malcolm Bangor-Jones's *Population Lists of Assynt 1638–1811* (Assynt Press, 1997) brings together six lists of names: the 1811 census (now held by the Highland Council), compiled by the schoolmaster and (breaking the rules) giving householder's names; a 1774 population list from John Hume's *Survey of Assynt* (NLS Dep. 313/1697 (Sutherland Papers); a 1746 list of heritors and parishioners who did not join the Jacobites in 1745, compiled by the minister (NLS, Saltoun Papers); the 1691 Hearth Tax (NAS E69/23/1), and two lists generated from the legal wranglings of the MacLeods chiefs of Assynt and the MacKenzies, who wanted to seize their land in return for unpaid debts; a 1667 list of tenants and proprietors derived from a Horning (NAS GD305/1/155/71); and a 1638 list of tenants and occupiers, from a Discreet of Removing in the

Court of Session (NAS CS7/505 ff.63v-65v). Some of these include patronymics, such as 'John MacLeod alias macNeil', John MacLeod son of Neil MacLeod, but in most cases the only genealogical clues are where people lived.

Assynt was inherited by the MacLeods of Lewis in the fourteenth century and was ruled from the early fifteenth century by a line of chiefs descended from Norman, second son of Roderick, sixth MacLeod chief of Lewis. In June 1672, the MacKenzies obtained 'letters of fire and sword', and besieged their castle of Ardvreck, and forced them to surrender.

The later lists show many more MacLeods than the earlier ones, with a particular jump between 1691 and 1746: evidence of people simply taking the MacLeod name, perhaps? Besides natural increase in population, though, the later lists seem to become more inclusive: that of 1746, for example, names all non-Jacobite men able to bear arms, so is necessarily far more complete than the 1691 hearth tax, which only names householders who were not exempt from paying due to poverty. Some MacLeods may have come in from elsewhere, but there is no recorded reason for immigration, and if anything you'd think MacLeods in this period would want to leave. As the MacLeod surname existed here earlier, there's no sensible reason for looking outside Assynt for the origins of its later inhabitants. Finally, as the MacLeods had lost their power to the MacKenzies, it seems pretty unlikely that anyone would adopt the surname for any expectation of gain. It seems likely, therefore, that the MacLeods in nineteenth-century Assynt were of the blood of the original chiefs.

My particular interest was in the family of Ally Alistair MacLeod, crofter in Badnaban, Assynt. His grandfather Angus MacLeod married Margaret MacLeod in Assynt on 14 November 1807. Margaret died at Badnaban on 14 February 1870, aged 88, so was born about 1780, when her parents were named as Alexander MacLeod and Catherine Matheson. Having placed a short account of Ally Alistair's life on my website, I was contacted by Roddy MacLeod, who is descended from Margaret's brother Roderick. He told me that, in the 1960s, Kenneth MacLeod, MBE, of nearby Inverkirkaig had recorded some oral tradition, that this same Alexander was born at Bad na h'Achlais. Hume's *Survey of Assynt* shows that Bad na h'Achlais was a sheiling (a summer encampment where the people went to graze their cattle) on the farm of Cnocaneach. Cnocaneach was 1½ miles (2.4 km) east of Badnaban, and I already knew that families had been cleared from Badnaban to Badnaban.

This placed Ally Alistair's ancestors back in Cnocaneach in the late eighteenth century. The next challenge was to find a plausible route back through the various population lists, one that did not involve ludicrous jumps, or far-fetched assumptions, to the clan chiefs.

The 1774 list includes an Alexander MacLeod, possibly our man, as a tenant farmer on a conjoint tack at Dubh Chlais, a mile (1.6 km) north-east of Cnocaneach. Cnocaneach itself was occupied by four families, of whom three were MacLeods, and presumably his relations, Roderick MacLeod, his son Roderick MacLeod, and Roderick MacLeod MacAngus (i.e. Roderick MacLeod, son of Angus MacLeod). We know Alexander was born on the farm of Cnocaneach: as his daughter Margaret was born in 1780, he was probably born about the 1750s or early 1760s. The 1746 list combined Cnocaneach and neighbouring Drumswordlin, and shows eight MacLeods, of whom one was probably his father:

- Rorie MacLeod
- Murdo MacLeod souldier
- Alexander MacLeod souldier
- John MacLeod alias MacOnil souldier
- John MacLeod alias macNeil souldier
- Angus MacLeod souldier
- Alexander MacLeod alias Maclein
- Angus MacLeod alias MacAnnish

Rorie is the Gaelic equivalent of the Norman name Roderick. Alexander named his eldest son Roderick, so this was probably his father's name, and here we have a Rorie in 1746 (though all the foregoing were probably very close relatives).

The 1691 hearth tax does not list any MacLeods at Cnocaneach, Drumswordlin, or Dubh Chlais. As people moved about as leases were granted and expired, it makes sense to see where Rorie et al's forbears may have been. The MacLeods in Assynt were:

- Culag: Rorie McLeoid 1
- Leadbeg: Alexander McLeoid 2
- Knockan (not the same as Cnocaneach): John McLeoid 1

This can't possibly be a comprehensive list of MacLeod householders in Assynt at the time. All the same, Rorie MacLeod of Culag, an old farm barely a mile (1.6 km) north-west of Cnocaneach, is at least a *plausible* ancestor for the MacLeods at Cnocaneach, where the name Rorie/Roderick remained in use for the next century.

The 1667 list, compiled before the MacLeods' fall from power, shows the following of their name in Assynt:

- Elfin: John McCleud brother of the Laird of Assint
- Culag: Rorie McCleud
- Achmelvish: Alexander McCleod
- Claichtoill: Neill Mccleod
- Stoir: Angus McCleod bailzie of Assynt
- Oldini: John and Neill McCleods
- Ardivar: Johne McCleod

Culag was somewhat removed from the conflict at Ardvreck and the presence of an earlier Rorie there suggests a degree of continuity. In 1638, we have:

- Donald mccleod alias neilsone of assint
- Fingoll [Florence] mcleod relict of umqll Neil mccleod alias neilsone of assint
- Neil mccleod her sone and appeirand air
- Alexander Mccleod in Torbreck
- Florence Mccleod in In[v]erchirkak
- Hew mccleod in loch beanache

As with the 1667 list, we have several people identified as members of the chief's family. The others were presumably his kinsmen, holding their tacks in return for military service. Rorie and Culag are not mentioned, but the pedigree of the chiefs themselves does include a Rory, a younger brother of Neil (1592–1633), whose widow Florence and son Neil *do* appear in the 1638 list, as does their father Donald Ban, Chief of Assynt. Nothing is known of this Rory, so he *could* have been identical with the Rorie who was in Culag by 1667, or else (say) his father or grandfather.

This is a tenuous connection, of course: the aim was never to produce a proven pedigree, as it was clear from the start that this would never be possible. But rather than giving up, this exercise provides a plausible route back through the few records that *are* available, and shows how one part of Assynt's later population could well have been, as they no doubt believed themselves to be, descendants of the MacLeod chiefs of Assynt.

In conclusion

This is just one example of how it can be possible to reconstruct a fine genealogy, tracing back to the origins of one of the great Scottish families, having started with only a few memories of great-grandparents. Exploring Scotland's antiquity has become easier with the appearance of the 'Paradox of Scotland' website, **www.poms.ac.uk**, that claims to include all Scots whose names survive in written records, such as charters, for the period 1093 to 1286.

Let me end *The Scotsman's* special, abridged version of my book *Tracing Your Scottish Family History* (Collins, 2008) by wishing you the best of good fortune in your own journey back into your Scottish family history.

Sources for clans

The pedigrees of many clan chiefs who received baronetcies or noble titles are in old editions of *Burke's Peerage*. The final printed version of *Burke's Peerage* (2003) for the first time included the pedigrees of all the clan chiefs recognized by Lord Lyon.

- **www.scottishamericansociety.org/id23.html** A handy list of the origins of Scottish clans.
- **www.gsi.org.uk** The Gaelic Society of Inverness journals contain some new research on clan origins.
- **www.celts.org/clans** Mainly Irish, but includes some Scottish clans e.g. MacLeod.
- **www.electricscotland.com/webclans/clanmenu.htm** A list of clans recognized by Lord Lyon, providing brief histories and links to websites. Electric Scotland's home, the Odom Library, Moultrie, GA, USA, houses the archives of 135 clan societies.